Magic for Everyone

Anytime and Anywere
(a comprehensive guide to prestidigitation)

MARIO BERARDELLI
(RUBEN)

 www.trafford.com

North America & international
toll-free: 1 888 232 4444 (USA & Canada)
fax: 812 355 4082

CONTENTS

INTRODUCTION

I think magic is by far one of the most interesting, enjoyable means of expression and in my opinion, vastly superior to any other hobby. There are many reasons for this enthusiasm. It involves communication, because it's exciting, because it requires skills and creates an open mind. It's just plain fun. This art form is linked to a tradition which is rich in culture, history and as old as mysterious as man. Most important, magic is a creative art form, one that will give you endless pleasure for yourself and your friends. Young or old, male or female, the success you enjoy is only limited to how far your eyes can see. The amount of ingenuity and creativity you can muster and the time plus effort, are your choices. This book can help you become involved and make you go as far as you want to go.

ABOUT THE AUTHOR

Mario Berardelli's spirits soar when asked to do a magic trick. The reason for this enthusiasm is his magic and showmanship. Mario Berardelli in art "RUBEN" arrived in U.S. in the late 60's.

Having been exposed to art at an early age, he soon found his love and interest in magic at the age of ten. At sixteen he enters the field with paid shows for birthdays, schools and holiday events. While in high school, he reaches the Yogi magic art and club, Baltimore's very best. This gives him a big leap into the magic scene which leads him to perform in the Baltimore-Washington areas including the L'enfant park hotel and governors club. By this time he meets Ray-Mond Corbin a past president of SAM and IBM and now in the Magic Hall of Fame. Ray-Mond becomes his personal teacher and mentor. Berardelli (Ruben) has been on American and European TV. He's performed for NATO's military, royalty and sports figures. He is currently in Europe where he continues his teaching and performances in cabaret style.

ABOUT THIS BOOK

Every trick selected had to be practical and no manipulative move was required. A means of eliminating the difficult move had to be created to present you with variety of tricks using only common articles that are easily obtainable. Any special apparatus required must be simple enough to be made by the average person or child. Also, any material thereof, must be easily obtainable. For example, in the kitchen, garage, around the house and in a hobby shop, just to name a few. These tricks are also created for every conceivable situation, wherever you find yourself, anytime and everywhere. Although non manipulative skill is involved, please study these tricks carefully before presenting them and never do a trick twice.

TIPS

The following points should be used as a guide for self-preparation of the enclosed material.

➢ BE NATURAL:
Work slowly deliberately and naturally.

➢ WATCH YOUR ANGLES:
Those are the site lines between the object you have and the spectators eyes. If these angles are not right, your audience may glimpse the object and expose your secret.

➢ NEVER REPEAT A TRICK
It's dull and boring. Beside, your audience may find out the secret. As we say in magic, leave your audience wanting more.

➢ PRESENTATION:
Your presentation should be simple and easily to understood, so your audience can fully understand the meaning of execution.

➢ PATTERN:
You must decide to be either funny or serious. First, you can simply describe what you are doing. Second, you may weave little stories around a particular trick. It only depends on your personality. Keep your audience interested in following your descriptions.

➢ DON'T TELL
The secret is only yours, and don't have to show a trick until you don't feel ready. Always practice and if possible, have your family to help you when you do so, they are your best audience. Do not practice in front of a mirror, it's not a live audience.

AKNOWLEDGEMENTS

Mark Wilson
Harlan Tarbell – The Tarbell Course
Joshua Jay
John Scarney – Scarney's Magic Tricks
Charles Berry Townsend – Worlds Best Puzzles
John Mulholland – Magic Of The World
Silvan – Silvan's Super Magic
Bob Long – Worlds Best Card Tricks
John Fisher – Never Give A Sucker An Even Break
George Shindler – Magic With Everyday Objects
Gen. Grant – O' Neal Magic
My Own Versions – Of Course

SPECIAL THANKS TO:

My wife Lina – Assistant and show coordinator;
My Sons Pasquale and William – Back Stage;
My Daughter Giusi – My Best Magic Trick;
My Mon and my Dad, who put up with me and said: "Stop this nonsense and do your homework";
My Teacher and Adviser Mr. Ray-Mond Corbin. Past President of IBM and SAM, and introduced into the Magic Hall Of Fame.
My friends Libera Illiano and Giacomo Esposito of Max Power Service.

And Thanks to all the magicians around the world.

CARDS

➤ YOU DO AS I DO

MATERIAL:
Two identical decks of cards.

PRESENTATION:

1. Take a deck of cards for yourself and hand the other to a spectator. Tell them to do as you do.
2. Mix the cards.
3. Exchange the decks.
4. Again mix the cards.
5. Exchange the decks.
6. Each of you pick a card from your pack, look at it and place it on top of deck.
7. Cut the cards once.
8. Exchange the cards again.
9. Find your selected card and place it face down on the table.
10. Show your card and ask the same of the spectator. Both cards will be identical.

SECRET:
When you and the spectator exchange cards to re-mix them note the bottom card of his deck. Exchange decks again. Choose your card and have the spectator do the same, remembering the bottom card of his deck as the key card. Have the spectator place is choice on top of the cards as you do. Now, both of you cut the cards and exchange them again it is now a matter of finding he key card with the one in front of it being the chosen one. Have both card placed on the table face down, one beside the other. Each of you turn your card over. You made a perfect match.

➤ ABOUT FACE

MATERIAL:
A deck of playing cards.

PREPARATION:
Secretly reverse the bottom card of deck with left hand.

PRESENTATION:
Place deck upon left hand, face down, the reversed card being next to the palm. (Figure 1)

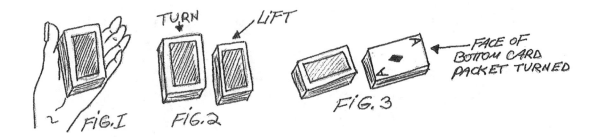

With the right hand lift up half of the cards. (Figure 2)
Bring right hand, with cards, over to the right, while showing face of bottom card. (Figure 3)
Just as right hand exposes card, the left hand turns over towards your body. (Figure 3)
The turning of both packets is very illusive. The reversed bottom card is now at the top. The spectator thinks he sees the real top of that packet. However, the cards are facing the same way. The packets of figure 3 are brought together.
The left cards are placed over the right about half way (Figure 4)

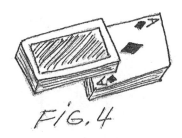

4

With the right thumb push down the right hand packet. (Figure 4 and 5)
Riffle the top half of the deck to show faces towards audience. The maneuver proves that half of the deck faces one way, and the other half the opposite. Grasp deck with right hand so that first two fingers are on reversed card and thumb is on the other side of deck. Reverse the deck. This brings the reversed card on the right. Reverse deck two more times. In all you have reversed three times. With the right hand pull up the reversed bottom and top car. (Figure 6)

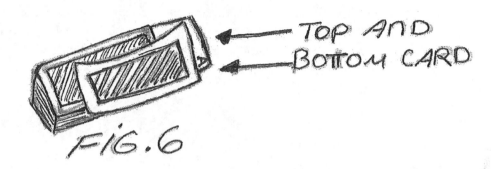

TOP AND BOTTOM CARD

FIG. 6

Show these cards to be facing opposite each other. Back of deck is towards audience. Place the two cards in the deck the same way, backs towards audience. Cards are now facing one direction. Fan or spread cards on table. You have finished.

➤ TURNABOUT

MATERIAL:
A deck of cards.

PRESENTATION:
Consign a deck of cards among three spectators. Have them each selected card. Take back the deck of cards and ask them to exchange their selection while your back is turned. Now turn your back again, with the deck in hand and ask to each spectators to insert their card into the deck. As you say this, place the cards on the table and spread them open. The selected cards will be face up, the rest of the deck, instead, will be face down.

SECRET:
When your back is turned, secretly turn around the last card of the deck. (Figure 1)

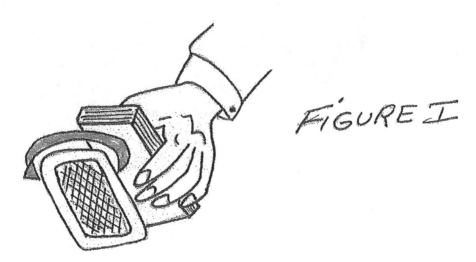

FIGURE I

At this point you ask the spectators to insert their cards. Before you spread the cards be sure to let fall the last card which was turned over in figure 1. Act normal, as though a natural mistake took place. Leave the card and proceed with the ending.

HOMING ACES

MATERIAL:
A pack of 52 cards.

PRESENTATION:
Take four aces from a pack, show them and place them face down on the table. On top of each, deal three cards face down. Set aside the rest of the cards. Place the piles one on top of the other, forming one pile. Explain that every fourth card is an ace. Fan the cards to show it is true. Now, even up the cards. From the top, deal four cards in a row, saying "What is this card?". You ask, tapping the ace with card in your hand. The spectators will say it's the ace. Regardless, ask to a spectator to turn it over, while you casually place the card in your hand on the bottom of the pack. Turn the ace to face down. Deal a row of cards on top of the cards you just dealt, saying "one, two, three, ace". Deal the rest of the packet in the same manner, again, "one, two three, ace". At this point, the spectator believes the aces to be in the fourth pile. Actually, the bottom one of the third pile is ordinary, while the other three in that pile are aces. Pick up piles one and two, and drop them on the deck. Take the ace from the original fourth pile and place it face up in front of that pile. Take the ordinary card from the bottom of the original third pile and place it face up in front of that pile. You now say "one pile of aces", and "one pile of ordinary cards". Say "I will make them change places". Wave your hands over the packs. First turn over the three ordinary cards and turn over the aces.

BETWEEN ONE AND TEN

MATERIAL:
A deck of playing cards.

PRESENTATION:
Give a deck of cards to a spectator and ask him to shuffle it well. Be sure to note and remember the bottom card. Let's say it is the five of clubs.

Ask the spectator to choose a number between one and ten. Suppose he chooses a five. Have him fan the cards and count down from the top five cards, the fifth card will be the chosen one. he doesn't have to tell you the card or number. (Figure 1)

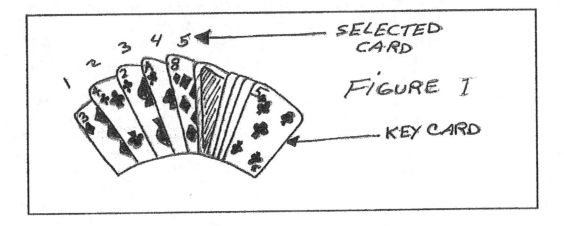

Have spectator square up the cards and cut them once. Have him count down the cards on the table in the same number of piles as the number he chose. In this case the example is five. (Figure 2)

Ask the spectator to pick up the piles in any order assemble them into a deck. Have him give you the cards. You take the deck and fan the cards towards yourself. Look for the keycard, "the five of clubs". (Figure 3)

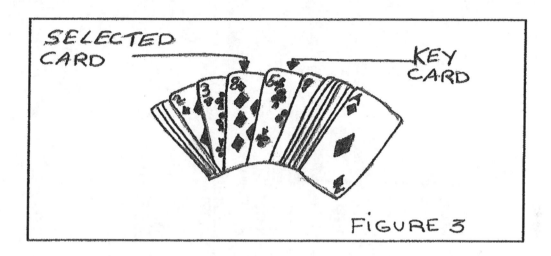

FIGURE 3

The card next to the five of clubs at the left side is the selected card, "the eight of diamonds".
When the spectator dealt the cards in piles, the caused the selected card and key card to come together.
Fan the cards towards yourself, be sure they are well separated in the vicinity of the chosen card. Bring the fan up and towards the spectator. Ask him to touch any card. Execute his movement deliberately and without haste.

THIRTY ONE BET

(For two Players)

MATERIAL:
A deck of 52 cards.

PREPARATION:
From a pack of cards remove all the spot cards from ace through six, twenty cards in all. Arrange them on a table as in the figure.

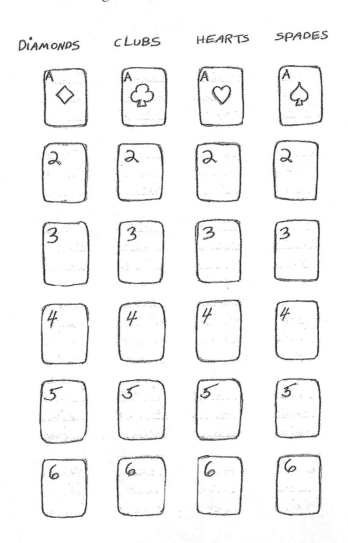

Both players take turns in turning one card face down, adding the values of the cards turned as they do so. Whoever reaches thirty one first, wins. Once a card is turned face-down it is out of play. If a player is forced over thirty one, he loses.

SECRET:
Have no fear, you can win every time just remembering a simple series of numbers. The sequence is 3, 10, 17, 24. A progression of 7 from 3, i.e. 3, 3+7 or 10, 10+7 or 17, 17+7 or 24.

PRESENTATION:
Should the opponent commence the game by turning over any card higher than 3 in value, you turn a card which will bring the total level with your second key number, which is 10. If the opponent turns a 6, you turn a 4. He might them turn a 3, for a total of 13, in which case you would turn a 1, making a total of 18, you then turn a 6, this gives you a 24, the final key number.

Whatever card he turn next, there's no way he can score 31 on his next move, where as you hit the target on yours.

Should the opponent turn 1 or 2 on his opening move, bring the total to 3, your first key, on yours; should he turn a 3, don't worry and try to hit a key number as soon as possible.

Should you play first, turn your first key 3, Whatever your opponent turns second, you'll always hit your key in an easy stride.

Should the opponent for one reason or another latch on the idea, work the following.

Allow him to turn a key number 3. You follow with another 3 for a total of 6. The sucker will now turn 4 to make first key 10. You follow with another 4, mailing 14, he must turn a 3 to produce a key of it. You produce another 4, for a total of 28, the sucker is speechless. There is no turn for a 31. He must turn a 1 or a 2. Just add the other total 31. You win.

ODDS OR EVEN

MATERIAL:
A deck of cards;
A simple knowledge of mathematics.

PRESENTATION:
Give a spectator a deck of cards and have him a separate a small portion. Have him count them and without looking, remove another portion for yourself.
Announce that the spectator has taken an "even" amount and that adding yours the number will be odds. Vice-versa if the spectators cards are odds, with yours added, will be even.
No matter how, you will always win.

EXPLANATION:
Be sure to always have an odd number of cards.
Example:

1. You have three cards, the spectator has eight. Eight plus three is eleven: Odd.
2. You have three cards, the spectator has seven. Seven plus three is ten: Even.

➢ AN OPTICAL ILLUSION

MATERIAL:
A deck of cards.

PRESENTATION:
Begin by placing the seven of clubs on the bottom and the eight of clubs on top of a deck.
Place the seven of spades and eight of clubs in such a way to be easily found.
Give the other two cards to your spectator, being the seven of spades and the eight of clubs. Have the two cards noted and placed in the deck at random, ad you now pick up the cards squeeze them in your hand and as you throw them face down unto the table retain the top and the bottom cards. It may sound difficult but a couple of tries will get you through. Show these cards to your spectator, and watch his amusement. The will not be able to distinguish the difference.

➢ I SEE SPOTS

MATERIAL:
A pair of good cutting scissors or a stiff razor;
A deck of cards;
A good adhesive tape;
A stiff card board white on both sides;
A red marker fine to medium point. Thus you can create two different sizes.

PREPARATION:

1. Take an ordinary playing card, place it onto the white card, board a trace around the borders. Remove the playing card with the diamond pips and carefully remove them, you will need seven of them, take your glue and paste them as in Figure 1, two on one side and five on the other.

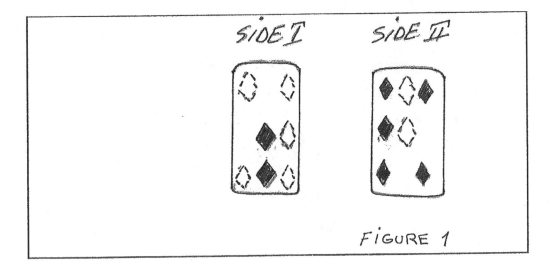

2. For a bigger more visual effect, construct the following. From the cardboard draw and cut a rectangle 4 ½ by 7".

Draw and color the diamond pips as in Figure 1, onto the cardboard, and your set to go.

14

PRESENTATION:

With an opportune positioning of your thumb or fingers on the pips, turn the cards five times, the audience will believe to see the three, six, ace and four of diamonds. With the left hand begin by covering the bottom most pip of the two of diamonds, thumbs on top and fingers underneath. The right thumb is turned to face the bottom center of the card, fingers on top. You are now showing an ace of diamonds and ready to begin. As you're turning and showing each face, the right hand turns the card one way towards the front, while the left hand turns it length wise towards the left side. Experiment and work with it a few times, you'll soon get the gist of it, your audience will be amazed.

RED AND BLACK'S

REQUIREMENT:
A simple mathematical calculation.

MATERIAL:
A complete deck of fifty-two cards.

PRESENTATION:
Have spectator shuffle the deck. Take the cards and begin dealing into a face-down pile. When you've dealt fifteen or more, ask the spectator to stop you whenever he wishes.
As you deal, count the cards to yourself. When spectator says stop, give him the dealt pile.
Ask him to choose, red or black. Suppose it is red, and further suppose that his pile contains twenty-three cards. You say: "I have three more red cards than you have black". Deal your cards face up, counting the black ones. You have three more red cards than he has black.
Have the spectator shuffle hi packet, and you shuffle yours. Take your original packet and begin dealing onto his, ask him to tell you when to stop. Again, keep track of the number.
Spectator had twenty-three, so you begin counting with twenty-four. When he tells you to stop. You again know the number of cards he has in his pile. Ask the spectator if he wants red or black. Suppose he chooses black, with thirty cards in his pile. The spectator how holds four more black cards than you have red. The spectator has four more cards than twenty-six.
However, always remember to deal from the larger to the small packet.

MECHANICS:
Take a deck of cards, shuffle it, and deal two piles of twenty-six cards each.
Suppose there are nineteen black cards in one pile.
You must also have seven black cards. So, no matter how you shuffle, the piles of twenty-six cards, will always have the same number of black cards in one pile as red in the other.
If you have twenty-six black cards in one pile, you will have twenty-six red cards in the other. The same holds true for twenty-five red cards and one black in your pile. The spectator now has twenty-five black cards and one red. Naturally, you have the same number of red cards as he has of blacks.
Remember to disguise the principal by using unequal piles and using a simple calculation.

FINAL THOUGHTS:
As above, the spectator had twenty-three cards.
That's three less than twenty-six. You therefore, have three more than twenty-six.
You now have three more red cards than he has blacks. Finally, you have three more black cards than he has reds.

SUPER-MONTE

MATERIAL:
Five playing cards (one must be a queen);
One bulldog clip;
Two inches long one wooden clothes pin peg.

PRESENTATION:
Take the five cards and place the queen of any suit in the center. Arrange them in a straight line. Trap the cards within the bulldog clip. (Figure 1)

FIGURE I

Stress the position of the queen. While holding the bulldog clip turn all cards over.
Ask the spectator to point to the queen and to mark it by placing the clothes pin over its end. (Figure 2)

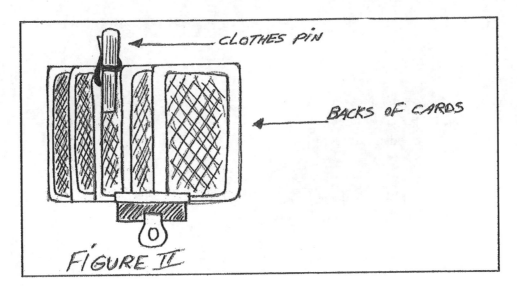

Now turn the cards over again, you won't believe your eyes. The peg will never appear to be where it should be, the spectator will believe it is on the queen, instead it always appears on the end card.

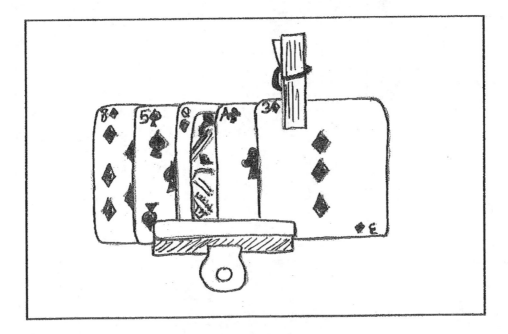

SECRET:
The secret depends up the discrepancy between the ways in which the cards overlap when placed face up and down. Just be sure the clothes pin is not too tight.

➤ I SEE RED

MATERIAL:
A deck;
A standard opaque envelopes.

PRESENTATION:
From a Deck remove five cards. Four being spades of clubs and one being hearts or diamonds. Place these five cards in their respective envelopes.
Be sure to overstate that the envelopes are opaque. Close and seal the envelopes and have them properly mixed. Take each envelope and one by one bring them close to your forehead while alluding to your telepathy; that you'll find the red card.

SECRET:
See Figures 1 and 2

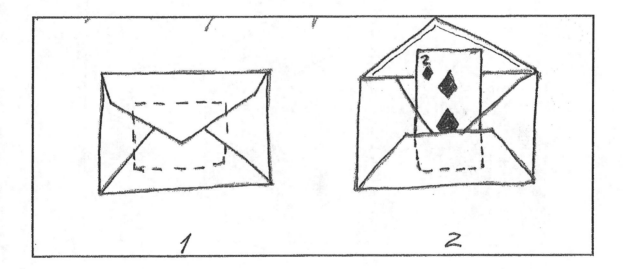

At the point of inserting the cards in the envelopes remember this:

1. Insert the four black cards horizontally.
2. Insert the one red card vertically.
3. Seal all envelopes.
4. Make your prediction.

➤ RISING CARD

MATERIAL:
A good deck of playing card;
One thin rubber band.

PRESENTATION:
Have a card selected and signed at the top.
Replace it in the deck. Ask the spectator to concentrate, this card will slowly rise out of the deck.

PREPARATION:
Take two cards and place a small hole in the center of each. Insert the rubber band and make a knot on each end. Place these two cards in the center of the deck. (Figure 1)

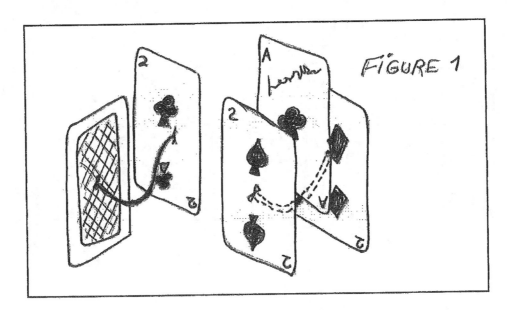

FIGURE 1

NOTES:

1. Often check the rubber band for possible dry rot.
2. Be sure the selected card is well placed in the center ad figure 1.
3. Grasp the cards as in figure 2.
4. Slowly release the crip and watch the selected card rise. (Figure 2)

➤ EQUILIBRIUM

MATERIAL:
A good deck of cards;
Good transparent tape;
Pencil, scissors and ruler.

EFFECT:
A glass tumbler is shown to be balanced on top of a card, which is standing upright.

PREPARATION:
Take the two jokers from the deck and place one aside. Take the other card with back towards you, and vertically devoid it in half. (Figure 1)

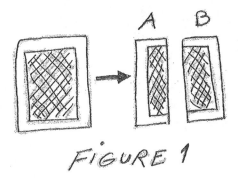

FIGURE 1

Be sure the vertical cut is straight and clean. Tape aside A or B onto the whole card, balks toward you the tape runs the entire height of the card. (Figure 2 shows the steps)

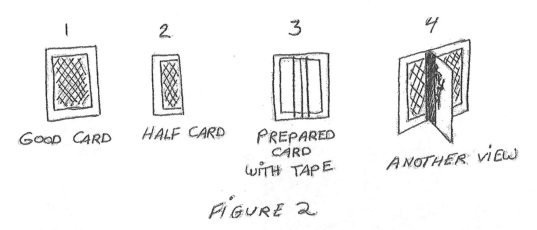

| 1 | 2 | 3 | 4 |
| GOOD CARD | HALF CARD | PREPARED CARD WITH TAPE | ANOTHER VIEW |

FIGURE 2

Figure 2, step 4, shows position of tape, Tahiti crates hinge like partition. Tape areas has been darkened for a better view.

PRESENTATION:

1. Place trick card on top of deck, backs toward you. Fan the cards before the spectator being careful that the trick card does not swing open. (Figure 3)

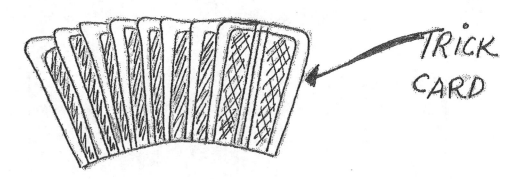

2. Close fan and casually remove the top card. Retain a grip on the hinged partition.
3. Discard the remaining cards on table.
4. You may show the trick card front and back. The secret cannot be detected form a short distance.
5. Pick up a glass tumbler, trick card in the other.
6. Place card upright letting the hinge open toward you.
7. Immediately place tumbler on the top of card and be sure it is well centered.

(Figure 4 shows front and back view)

FRONT VIEW

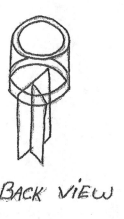

BACK VIEW

ACE SURPRISE

MATERIAL:
A deck of 52 cards;
A pair of Nail-Clippers.

PREPARATION:
Remove the four aces and trim a slight crescent from each of their top right and lower left face-up corners. (Figure 1)

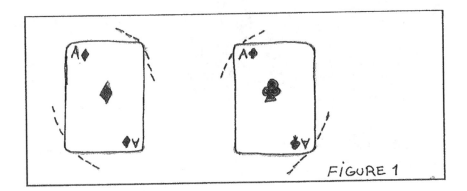

FIGURE 1

Make these cuts clean and round, and replace the back into the pack. If when you now riffle the outer left edge of the face down pack, you cannot instantly detect the cards, just make them a little deeper.

PRESENTATION:
Fan and show the cards, or simply spread them on table. Gather up the cards and remove the four aces. Give the rest of the pack to a spectator, who has to shuffle it. Ask to the spectator to remove the aces and loose them in the pack by shuffling. Finally, the cards are handed back to you. It is now a simple matter of riffling the outer left corner of the face down pack to find the aces. One at a time.

1. A slight break will occur when riffling.
2. Remember to add some drama to this presentation.

TIPS:
If you wish to make this experiment seem more impressive, trim the red and black aces in opposing corners, see the illustration. You would then have no difficulty in cutting to the aces in the order of colors called by the spectator.

MONEY

➤ COIN AND HANDKERCHIEF

MATERIAL:
A man's white pocket handkerchief;
A U.S. quarter or half dollar (You can also use €)

PREPARATION:
Fold the handkerchief in half like a triangle. While sitting in front of your spectators, spread it out on the table, so that the corners overhang the border. (Figure 1)

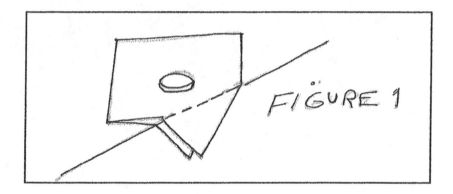

FIGURE 1

Wrap the coin inside the center, as in figure 1. Lift the opposite corner of the handkerchief as thought holding the coin fight. (Figure 2)

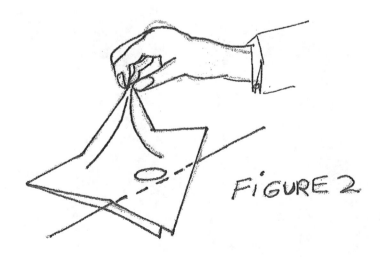

FIGURE 2

As you pull up the handkerchief towards yourself, let the coin fall on your lap.
Use a continuous flowing movement. Shake the handkerchief as thought the coin has vanished into the air.

SPECIAL NOTE:
While the hand shakes the handkerchief, the other one removes the lapped coin and produces it, in any way desired.

VANISHING DIME
(OR TEN CENT €)

MATERIAL:
2 U.S. half dollars (or €);
1 U.S. dime (or ten cent €);
A bit of bees wax.

PRESENTATION:

Put the half dollar on the table, place on it the dime and on top of that, the second half dollar. Pick up the little stack of coins by the edges between your right forefinger and thumb and hold it about 10 inches above your left hand, which you extend flat and palm upwards. Say: "I will now drop the half dollar and the dime, causing the dime to disappear as it falls. Release the lower coin. That half dollar falls flat on your hand, the dime has vanished. You show nothing in your hand but the other half dollar which you flick in the air, catch it and put it away.

SECRET:
Fix a tiny pellet of wax under your fingernail. At an opportune moment, press it on the dime. In putting the dime on the first half dollar, place this waxed side downwards with a slight pressure so that the two coins will adhere. (Figure 1)

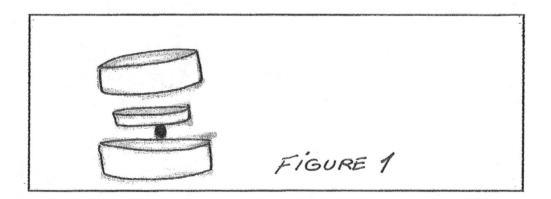

FIGURE 1

When you pick up the stack, this half dollar is below and when you let it drop, it will turn over, bringing the dime below it. (Figure 2)

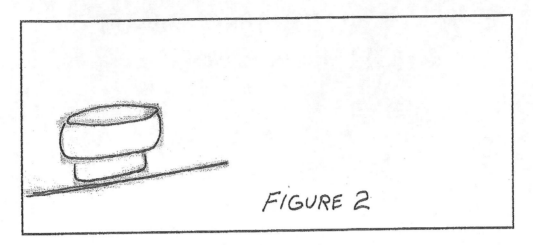

FIGURE 2

A moment later when you spin it in the air, the attached dime will be invisible and the double coin will fall on your hand, with the dime below. There is ample cover when spinning the coin.

WITHOUT THE HALF DOLLARS:

On the nail of the middle finger of your hand, put a pellet of soft wax. If you now place a dime on the palm of the same hand, laying it against the flashy lower part of your thumb and clench your fist tightly, you can press the dime tightly on the fingernail and, on opening your hand rapidly and spreading the fingers wide apart, show hand perfectly empty.

RING AND COIN

MATERIAL:
Two rye rings;
A piece of cardboard;
Two sheets of eight and one-half inch by eleven inch of white paper.

EFFECT:
A borrowed coin is placed flat on the table near two key rings and two small squares of cardboard. One cardboard square is placed over one of the key rings.

These rings and square are stacked on top of the other piece of cardboard; the ring and squares of cardboard are stacked on top of the remaining ring, and the entire stack is placed over the borrowed coin. The performer removes the top squares of cardboard, then the first ring, and the other square of cardboard, and reveals that the coin which was in center of the remaining ring has vanished. Restacking the ring and the coin is made to re-appear.

PREPARATION:
To determine if the cardboard is the proper size, place one of the squares on one of the key rings. The rim of the ring should protrude from all sides of the square, but you should be unable to see anything inside the ring. Apply glue to one surface of the sheets of paper to the ring.

When the glue has dried, cut away the excess paper, leaving a small circle glued to the underside of the ring. It should not extend beyond the perimeter of the ring.

GETTING READY:
When ready to perform the effect, place the other sheet of paper flat on the table with the ring and squares lying on the sheets of paper. In this way, the paper glued to one of the rings will not be visible. See illustration.

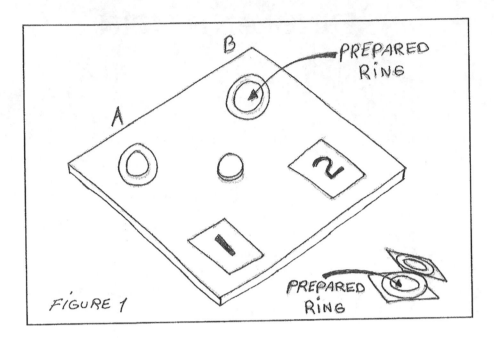

FIGURE 1

PRESENTATION:

Place a coin on the center of the sheet of paper. (Figure 1)

With your left hand, pick up "square 1", holding it with your thumb on one edge and your first two fingers on the opposite edge, holding the cardboard from above. Place "square 1" over "ring A" and pick up both in the manner described above. Place them on top of "square 2" and, adding this square to the stack, place them all on top of "ring B" (which is the prepared ring). Lift up the entire stack and place it on top of the coin. With your right hand, remove "square 1", placing it in the lower right-hand corner of the sheet of paper. Remove the ring from the stack and place it on top of "square 1". With the left-hand, remove "square 2", and place it in lower left-hand corner of the sheet of paper. The coin is now hidden under the circle of paper glued to "ring B". The coin has vanished.

To make coin re-appears again, pick up "square 1", with "ring A" on top of it, with your right hand. Place these on top of the prepared ring. Raise the prepared ring slightly off the paper, and with the left hand, slide "square 2" under the prepared ring, but over the coin. With the left hand, raise the entire stack and show that the coin has re-appeared.

INVISIBLE TRAVELER

MATERIAL:
Any U.S. penny, nickel, dime, quarter (or €)

EFFECT:
Two coins are picked up, one in each hand, and the hands are closed over them, forming fists. Two more are placed on the hands, one in each fists, at the finger tips. The fists are quickly turned over. A transference is found to have taken place. When the hands are opened, three coins are found in one, and only one in the other.

PRESENTATION:
Place four coins on the table. Pick up one in each hand, and keeping the palms up, close the fingers over the coins so as to form two fists. Ask the spectator to place a penny on each closed fist, right at the juncture of the fingertips and the palms. See figure.

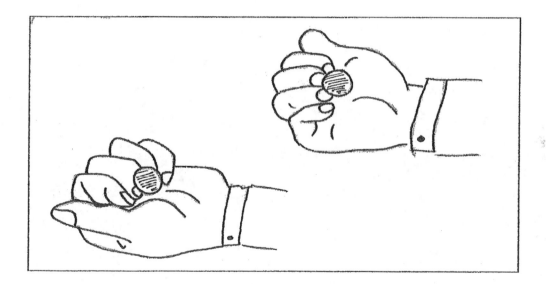

Rapidly turn over your fists. While turning both right and left hand inward, grasp the two outside coins. You have to do this move quickly. This is easily accomplished by opening your left fist approximately half an inch, and rapidly closing it again. At the same time, let both the coin that the spectator placed on your right hand and the coin enclosed in that hand, drop to the table. This should be done with no perceptible opening of the right fist.

The spectator must not know that both coins come from the same hand. You must ACT as though you've made a mistake, excuse yourself and have the coins re-placed on your fists. This bit of misdirection is a perfect cover. To strengthen this, keep the fists fairly close together, and by permitting the coins which was on your right hand to fall under your left hand.

Quickly turn the fists over again, drawing the coins into both fists in the same manner as you drew the coins into your left hand before.

Turn your fists and palm up again, open your hand slowly, and show one coin in the right hand and three in left. One coin has traveled from one hand to the other.

HEADS OR TAILS

MATERIAL:
One U.S. nickel (or €)

EFFECT:
The performer tells to a spectator to spin a coin on the table top. By mere concentration is able to tell whether the coin falls heads or tails.

PREPARATION:
Use a nickel, and with a sharp knife or file, upon one of its surfaces, right at the edge, make a fairly large nick, but not large enough to be seen. See figure.

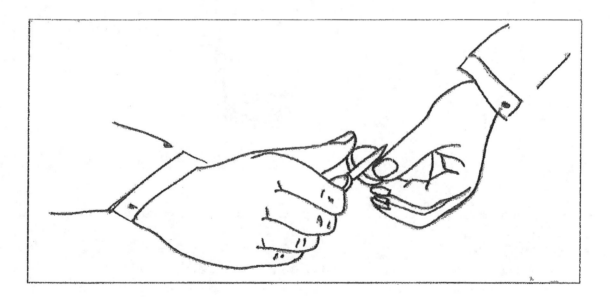

The sound of the nickel is different as it comes to rest. Spin yourself a few times and you will notice the difference. If the nick is on the tail side of the coin, when this comes to rest it sounds flat and clicky.
Therefore, the side that turns up is head. If the head falls, it will sound clear and ringing, and a spin will last slightly longer. Therefore, the coin will turn up tail.

CIGARETTE TO DOLLAR BILL (OR €)

MATERIAL:
One glass of water;
One dollar bill (or €);
One cigarette.

PREPARATION:
Remove the tobacco from the paper of a cigarette. Roll up a dollar Bill and place it within its paper so that it looks like a whole cigarette. Push the doll Bill well into the cigarette chamber. Take some left over tobacco and work it into the remaining space. Simulating a real cigarette. (Figure 1)

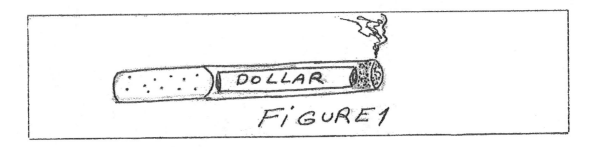

A cigarette thus prepared can be lit and shown to be real. Place the prepared cigarette in its pack.

PRESENTATION:
Say to your audience that you smoke the most expensive cigarettes in the world.
Remove a cigarette from a pack, light it or take one smoke (should you care to). Either case the cigarette must be lit. Now dip the cigarette in the glass of water to extinguish the lit portion. The cigarette must be immersed up to the filter. Remove it, placing it between your hands. Roll the cigarette briskly between the hands until all traces of the paper have gone. Unroll the dollar Bill, and show hands empty.

➤ UP AND DOWN

MATERIAL:
Any dollar bill (or €);

EFFECT:
The performer holds a dollar bill with its picture face towards the audience. By a series of simple folds and unfolds, without turning the bill over, the picture will appear upside down.

PRESENTATION:
Hold a dollar bill with its picture face towards the spectator, the picture upright. (Figure 1)

Fold the upper half of the dollar bill forward and down. (Figure 2)

Now fold the right half of the dollar bill forward and to the left. (Figure 3)
The bill is now folded into a packet of quarters.

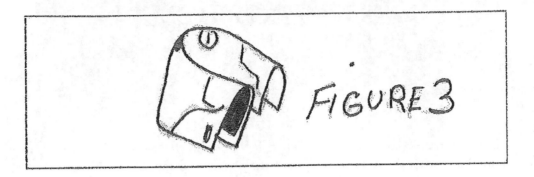

Fold the right half of the packet forward and to the left, forming a pocket of eights. The fold with the four corners are now towards a page backward, unfolding the dollar bill back into quarters. (Figure 4)

Now unfold the half of the dollar bill towards you, to the right, again as if turning a page, but this time to the left. Unfold the half of the dollar bill towards the audience, bringing it up and revealing that the picture has mysteriously turned upside down. (Figure 5)

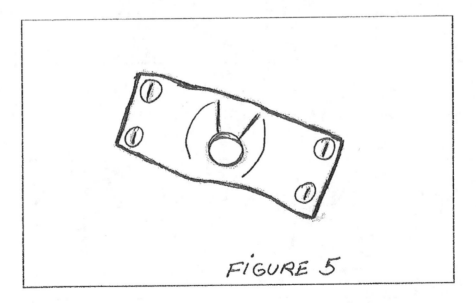

➤ FLYING DOLLAR BILL (OR €)

MATERIAL:
A dollar bill (or €)

PRESENTATION:
Hold a dollar bill in your right hand, at about chest level. Have someone place his left hand around the middle of the bill, with the thumb and first finger about an inch apart. "No part of the hand may touch the bill." See figure.

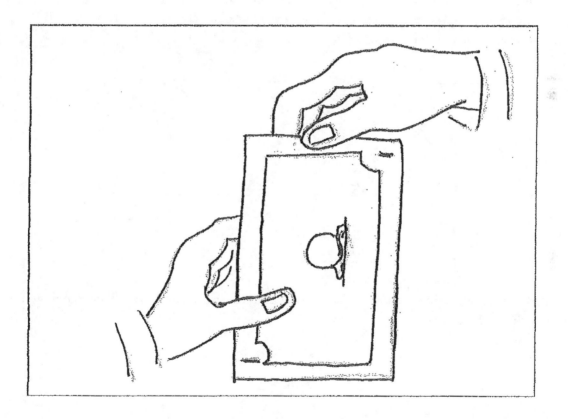

Tell your friend that when you'll let go the bill, he won't be able to catch it before it passes through his fingers.

SECRET:
Sounds easy. It's impossible to do it more than one in ten tries. Your reflexes are not just fast enough.

COIN THROUGH HANDKERCHIEF

MATERIAL:
A U.S. quarter or half dollar (or €);
A man's white pocket handkerchief.

PRESENTATION:
Hold coin between left thumb and fingers. Coin and hand are covered with the handkerchief. With thumb and fingers of right hand, fold coin and handkerchief over towards yourself. (Figure 1) Then hold the same, with left thumb and fingers through the handkerchief. (Figure 2)

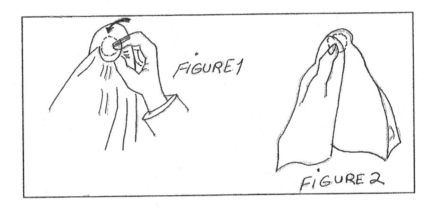

Corner C of handkerchief in now pulled up over coin on top of corner A, which exposes coin to the spectator. (Figure 3)

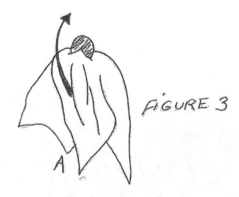

Instead of bringing corner C back over the coin, corner A is also brought up with it the spectator now believes that coin is now covered by handkerchief. In reality the coin is behind the center of the handkerchief. (Figure 4)

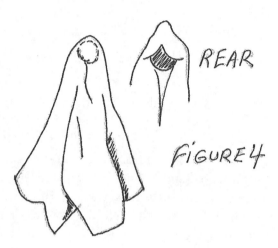

REAR

FIGURE 4

Twist the handkerchief around coin. (Figure 5)

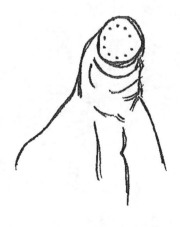

FIGURE 5

Remove by pushing coin through handkerchief with right hand. Open and show handkerchief unharmed.

➢ COIN VANISH

MATERIALS:
A white pocket handkerchief;
Any coin from a quarter to a penny (or €);
A bit of bees wax.

SPECIAL NOTE:
Before you begin place a bit of bees wax under the left thumb nail.

PRESENTATION:
Spread a pocket handkerchief on a table and place a coin in the center. As left thumb is on coin, right hand now brings first corner of handkerchief to cover coin. As the left thumb is covered, the right finger press on left thumb to extract the bees wax onto the coin.
At this point, the left thumb is withdrawn. The right thumb presses handkerchief onto the waxed coin, so as to make it stick. This is one continuous flowing movement. Let spectator feel coin through handkerchief. Cover coin with second corner of handkerchief. (Figure 1)

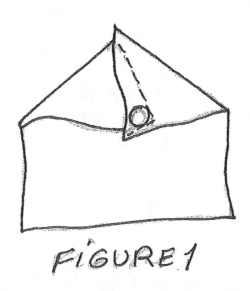

FIGURE 1

Bring up other two corners over coin, this forming an envelope. (Figure 2)

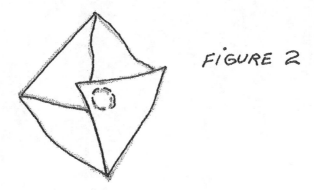

FIGURE 2

Open up side of Handkerchief nearest you and grasp edge with both hands. (Figure 3)

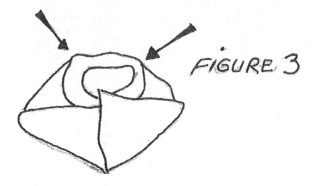

FIGURE 3

Pull hands apart, running them along the edge with both hands. As the coin is fastened to the corner of handkerchief it is automatically pulled into the right hand. (Figure 4)

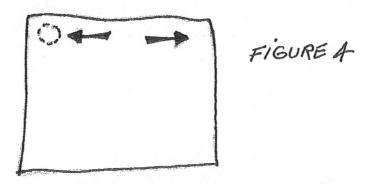

FIGURE 4

Arrows of Figure 4 show direction in which to pull. As this is done, handkerchief us raised off the table, given a shake, and allowed to hang down. Coin has vanished.

SILKS

Good to average silk handkerchief's can be found at your local 5 and 10 stores at reasonable prices. There are many varieties and colors. I recommend a small to medium size square and scarf's, these can be organ pleaded for small packing.

SILK FROM A MAGAZINE

METHOD #1

MATERIAL:
Some small silk squares or scarf;
One magazine;
Common household glue;
Scissors.

PRESENTATION:
Prepare a magazine, any monthlies will do, by removing the cover and cutting the pages diagonally from a point half way up the back to another point about half way across the bottom. Glue the cut edges together and then fasten the cover on again. (Figure 1)

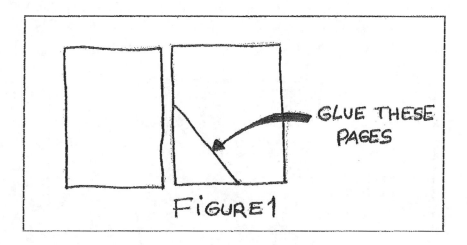

FIGURE 1

Fold a number of silks to fit the cavity, arranging the corner so that the silks can be pulled one by one. Take the magazine e ruffle the pages, the unprepared part towards the front. Roll it up into a tube, look through it at the spectator turn the prepare end upwards and pull out several of the silks. Unroll the tube, riffle the pages and repeat the production

SILK FROM A MAGAZINE

METHOD #2

MATERIAL:
Any magazine;
A soft silk scarf.

EFFECT:
A magazine of any kind is shown. The performer flips through the pages and asks a spectator to stop him. When the spectator says "stop", the performer offers to go forward, backward or remain at that page. The page is then torn from the magazine, and wadded into a ball. The performer tears into the paper and produces a colorful silk.

PREPARATION:
The silk is folded into a small size that can be concealed by the four fingers of one hand. Now, when ready to perform, simply pick up the magazine and silk together with one hand. The silk is held by the back cover and concealed by the four fingers of that hand. (Figure 1)

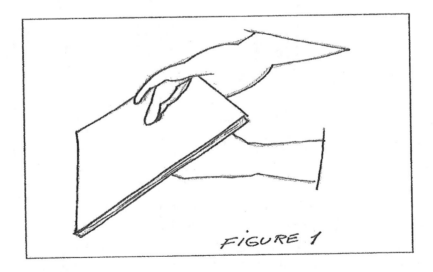

FIGURE 1

You then begin flipping through the pages and ask the spectator to stop you at his will. (Figure 2)

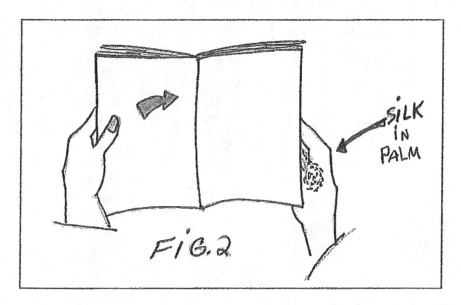

When he says to stop, offer to go forward, backward, or remain with that page. After the spectators has decided on a definite page, use the other hand to rip it from the magazine by pulling down. (Figure 3)

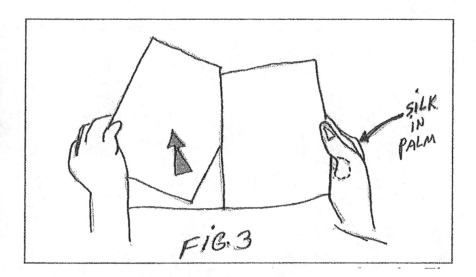

You then place the page back in place under your thumb, and pull the remainder of the magazine away with your other hand. (Figure 4)

FIG. 4

This leaves you with one page in hand and the silk still concealed behind it with your fingers. (Figure 5)

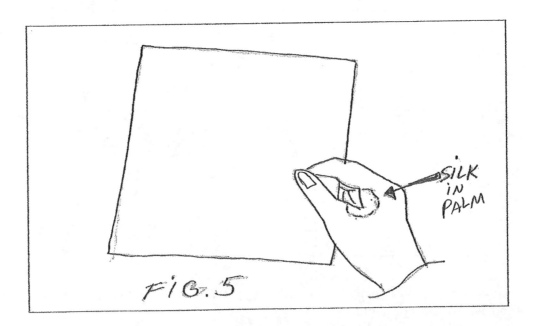

FIG. 5

Now, simply wad the paper into a ball around the silk. (Figure 6 and 7)

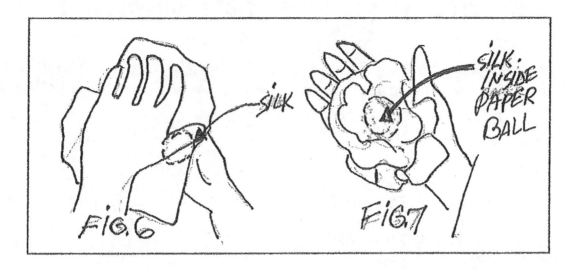

Tear the paper, reach in and grab a corner of the silk and pull it out. (Figure 8)

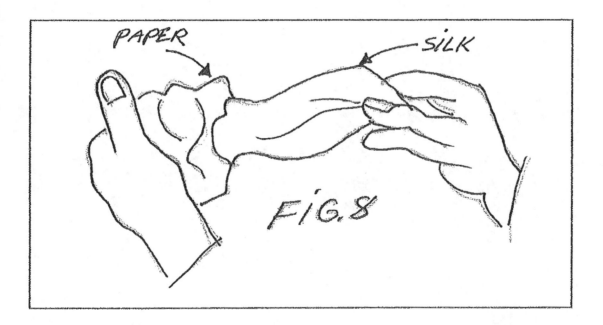

SILKS FROM NEWSPAPER

Here is another type of silk production that is rarely seen on the magic scene. Read it a few times. Practice and work with it more times, you'll have delighted your audience with beautiful magic. Oh! And so easy too!

MATERIALS:
A full page newspaper;
Match box, big enough to be hidden by the back of your hand;
A strip of soft metal half inch wide and four to five inches long, easily obtainable from a coke can;
Scotch tape, normal and double faced;
3 small silks that can easily fit into box;
One brush and tempera, skin tone.

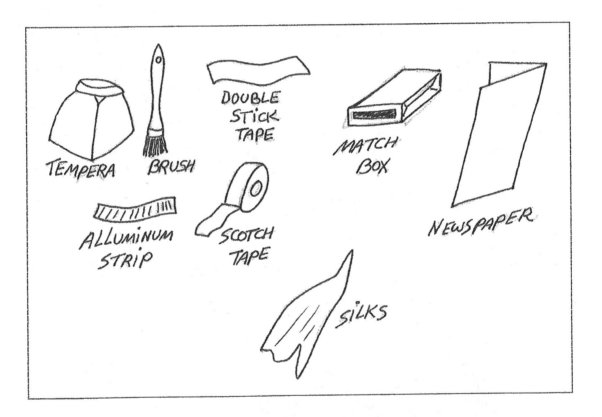

PREPARATION:
Bend the aluminum strip to fit your right hand as in Figure 1.

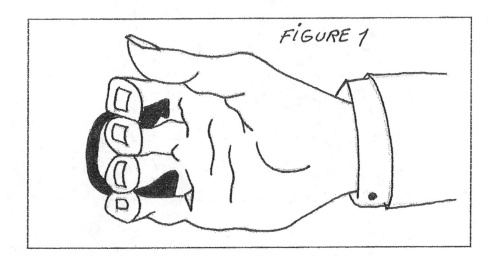

Take the match box and cut two openings on top of it. Insert the aluminum strip and tape the inside and outer parts. (Figure 2) Which we will call a servant.

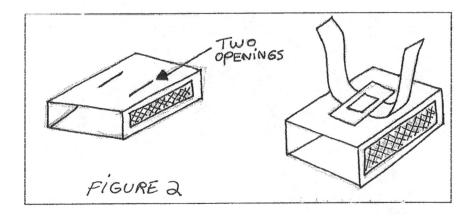

Paint all parts of this with tempera skin tone. Turn over the servants. Cut a piece of double scotch tape and apply to its surface. (Figure 3)

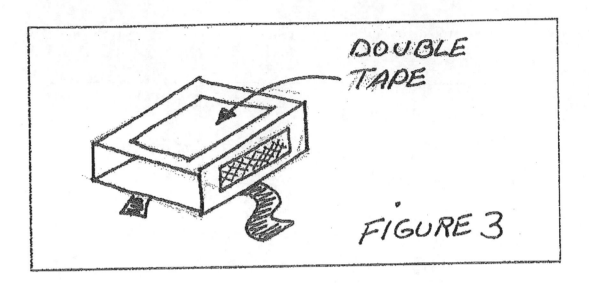

Introduce the first silk handkerchief in the servant being careful to leave one corner protruding. Wrap this corner to another silk and to a third. (Figure 4)

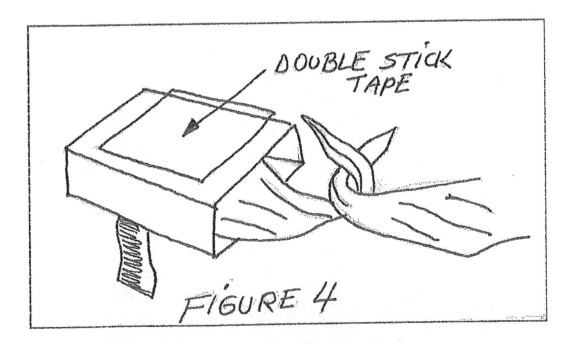

Push these silks well into the prepared box, you're set to go.

PRESENTATION:

Spread out the newspaper onto a table and being careful to corner the servant. As you approach the table to grasp the newspaper pick up the servant under cover with right hand. Figure 5 shows the proper position.

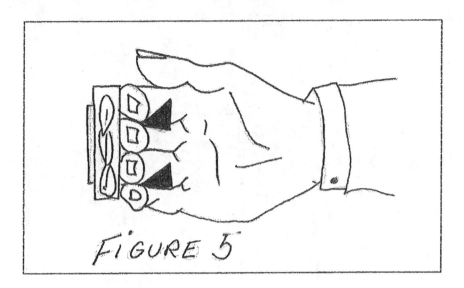

Stand in front of the spectator, open the newspaper and hold it vertically with the thumb and palm of the right hand. There by hiding the hand and the servant. (Figure 6)

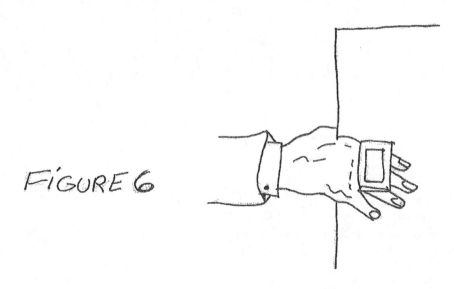

With the left hand grasp the inferior part of the news paper showing both sides. Your right hand releases the newspaper which fall on the left and immediately grasping it with the right hand which remains in the same position; thus, concealing the servant.

Move the right hand towards the center and bring the left to a point visible to the spectator.

Bore a hole in the newspaper with the first finger of your left hand. Bend the right fingers to its palm, thus positioning the opening of the servant to the newspaper. (Figure 7)

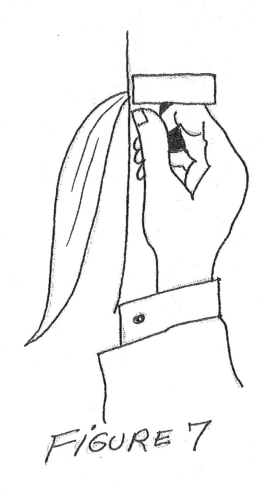

FIGURE 7

With the fingers of the left hand, push the newspaper against the right hand so that the thumb and first fingers can grasp a little of the newspaper.

With the first and thumb of the left hands being pulling the silk. Place these on the table.

Repeat this three times from different areas of the newspaper.

When all silks hand been produced turn toward left, face to audience and begin to fold the newspaper. The servant is now hidden within the newspaper which is then distracted from audience. (Figure 8)

FIGURE 8

DOUBLE TAPE

SYMPATHETIC SILKS

This is one of the oldies and widely used silk trick.

MATERIAL:
One bulldog clip;
6 very large silks.

EFFECT:
The apparent transfer of knots from one set of silks to another.

EXPLANATION:
Three red silk handkerchiefs are firmly tied by opposite diagonal corners. The blue silk handkerchiefs are not tied. By waving your hands over these silks, the knots are made to change places, from the reds to the blue ones.

PREPARATION:
Begin by tying the three blue silks by their opposite diagonal corners. Use small knots and lay them flat on the table. (Figure 1)

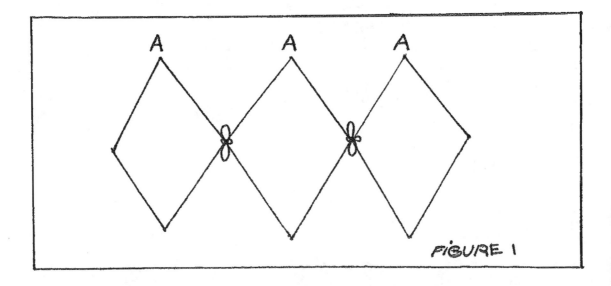

FIGURE 1

Gather them together so that the knots are hidden in the folds and put them in the fork of the left hand, gripping all them of the ends "A" by the thumb and forefingers; they may be secured by a small bulldog clip, which falls to the back of the hand. The other three silks remain separate, put these in front of the other three, all the ones protruding above the thumb and forefinger.

Call attention to the silks and proceed to count them one by one. Take the projecting end of the first, draw it up through the left hand, shaking it and counting "one". Draw the second away, counting "two". As the hands come together to take the third, bend the left third finger around the two just counted, release them from the right fingers and thumb, grip and draw away the three knotted silks and count "three". Properly timed the action is perfectly deceptive. Bundle these up and drop them on the seat of a chair. Count the three single ones in exactly the same way. Tie these together with a dissolving knot, as follows. Roll up together the opposite diagonal corners of the silks by a one "turn knot". (Figures 1, 2 and 3)

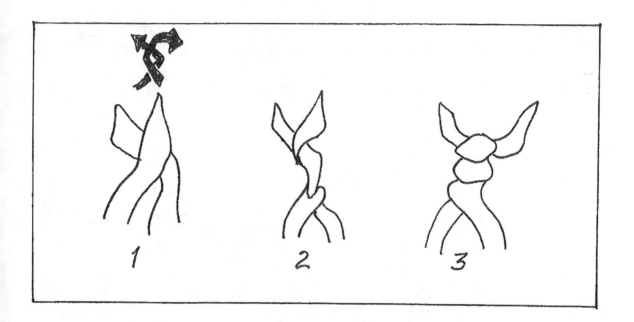

Rolling once, twice and applying a regular knot. Do not pull to tight. Drop these on a chair at the opposite side of the others. Pretend to transfer the knots from one set of silks to the other. Lift the three just tied, one by one, with a little shake and come apart. Lift one of the other corners and shake them out with, a whisk of the hand, showing them firmly knotted.

A NOVEL SILK VANISH

This particular method of vanishing a silk handkerchief is easy, clean and sure fire. In particular, it can be applied to the 20ᵗʰ century silks, which follow.

MATERIAL:
2 brown lunch bags;
A good household glue or cement;
Scissors;
Pencil and ruler if necessary.

PREPARATION:
Open the seams of one lunch bag, being careful not to rip any portion. (Figure 1)

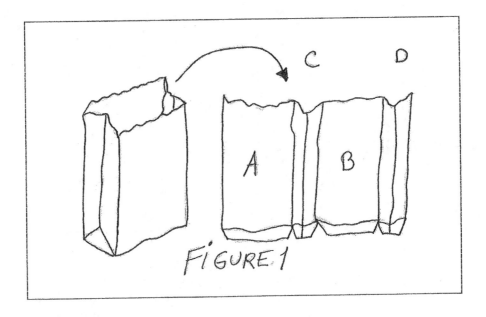

FIGURE 1

You now have two portions which we call panel "A" and "B". Also notice that panel "B" is between two columns, "C" and "D". It is panel "B" with column "C" and "D" that we will use. Cut away panel "A" and discard it. (Figure 2)

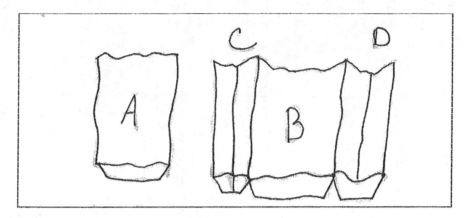

Discard half of "C" and "D", cutting in the seam. (Figure 3)

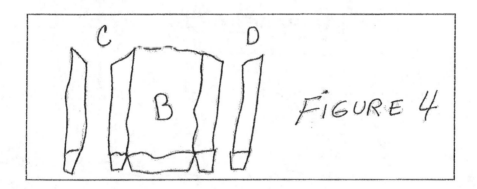

FIGURE 4

You will now have only portion "B" with part of "C" and "D" column. (Figure 4)
Snip off the two tongues of "C" and "D". (Figure 5)

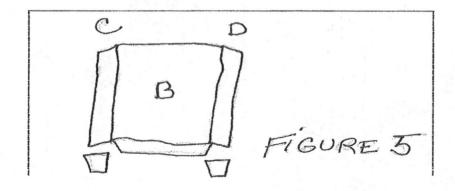

FIGURE 5

Discard these and you're set to prepare the secret part of the bag.
Apply the glue on the outside flaps of the panel "B". See shaded areas. The flaps are turned inward. (Figure 6)

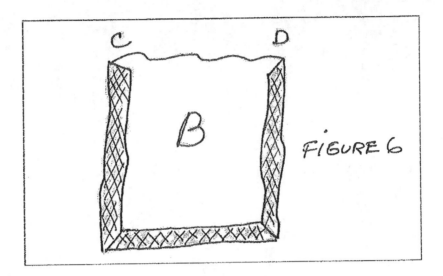

Carefully apply this prepared panel outside the other lunch bag being careful to match the inside wall. (Figure 7)

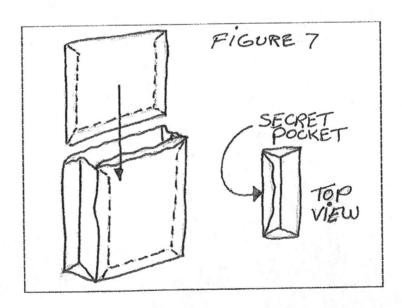

You have now created a secret compartment within the other lunch bag. This any silk handkerchief can be made to vanish; it's twin to be produced later.

The slight bulge, if any, is on the outside of the bag.

In other words, the pocket is actually on the outside of the bag… but the pocket opening is on the inside.

BASIC MOVES:

You first place a silk or silks in the bottom of the bag. Index finger and thumb of right hand is pressing down the opening of the bag so it does not bulge open. Turn bag upside down and show it empty being careful to keep the back of the bag towards you. Silk has vanished. You may reproduce it as in the 20th Century silks or any other way you wish.

➤ 20TH CENTURY SILK

Perhaps one of the most popular and recognizable trick with silk. The trick wherein a silk is vanished and reappears, knotted between two or other silk previously tied together. Here, I give you a way to prepare and perform this wonder of magic. Use if you can a 12 to 16 inch silks.

WITH UPREPARED SILK:
Tie three silk, say a red, a white and a blue, with small reef knots, and lay them out flat on the table (Figure 1, A)

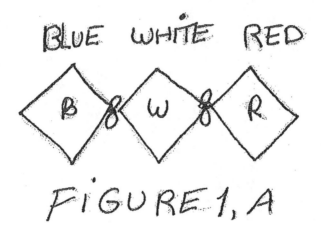

FIGURE 1, A

Fold the red over the white. (Figure 2, B)

FIGURE 2, B

Fold the three corners over to the middle. (Figure 3, C)

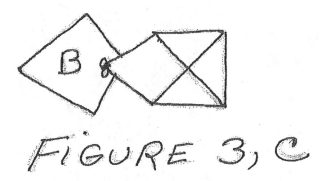

FIGURE 3, C

Turn these two silks inward in narrow folds to the middle. (Figure 4, D)

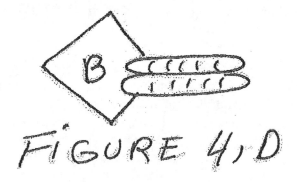

FIGURE 4, D

Hold the right hand corner of the blue and twist this roll round and round into a kind of rope. (Figure 5, E)

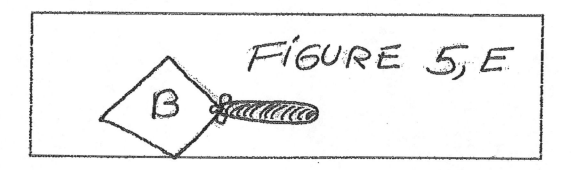

FIGURE 5, E

Lay the red and the white, thus "roped" along the upper right hand edge of the blue. (Figure 6, F/G/H)

FIGURE 6,F

Roll it up in the blue in the direction of the knotted line in "H". The blue may bow be shaken and no part of the red or white will show as long as it is held by the top corner.

PRESENTATION:
Show the blue, white and red silks tied together in a chain, the blue at the top. The knots are slip knots and you quickly detach the white and red from the blue which is given to a spectator to be held upright, top end in his right hand, bottom end in his left. Vanish the white and red, seize the blue by one of the side corners, shake it out and duplicate white and red silks appear instantly.

SILK PENETRATION

EFFECT:
The magician displays a drinking glass, holding it mouth up with the tips of his fingers. He then places a handkerchief into the glass and covers both this handkerchief and the glass with a second handkerchief. Next, he places a rubber band over the second handkerchief and the glass, thus sealing the first handkerchief inside the glass. Now, holding the glass from the outside, he reaches under the handkerchief for a brief moment and instantly withdraws the first handkerchief - the one that was sealed inside the glass! The outside handkerchief is removed and all may now be examined. AN IMPOSSIBLE PENETRATION!

SECRET:
In turning the glass upside down while it is being covered by the second handkerchief. Please maintain a safe distance between you and the audience.

PRESENTATION:
(1) Hold the tumbler mouth up, at the tips of the fingers and thumb of the right hand as in figure. (2) Now show a silk or handkerchief, this will be the one that later will penetrate the tumbler. Push the silk into the tumbler with your left hand. (3) Pick up the second handkerchief or silk with the left hand and bring it up in front of the glass, momentarily hide the glass from view.

THE SECRET MOVE:
(4) As you begin to cover the tumbler with the handkerchief-silk, your right hand slightly relaxes its grip on the bottom of the tumbler, allowing the tumbler to pivot between your thumb and fingers (5) until the tumbler has turned upside down.

NOTES:
(6) The handkerchief inside the glass should be large enough so it will not fall out when you turn the glass upside down.
As the tumbler turns over, your left hand finishes covering both the right hand and the tumbler, figure 7.
After the tumbler is covered, grip the glass through the cloth with your left hand as in figure 8. Remove your tight hand, casually showing it empty and pick up a rubber band from the table. Spread the rubber band with your right fingers and place it around the handkerchief-silk and the top of the tumbler (really the bottom) unknown to anyone, figure 9.
With the empty right hand reach, underneath the covering handkerchief-silk the one that is inside the glass. Pull it down into view-the handkerchief-silk has penetrated, figure 10.

Now with your right hand reach, underneath the covering handkerchief-silk and grip the tumbler to make the secret turn-over move this time with the mouth of the glass (which is at the bottom) between the tips of your right thumb and fingers, figure 11.

With your left hand grip the other (second) handkerchief-silk between the tips of the fingers at the very top of the covered tumbler and pull the cloth to release the rubber band, figure 12.

Now allow the tumbler to pivot in the fingers and draw the handkerchief-silk away from the hands, figure 13.

CORDS AND ROPES

MAGIC KNOTS

MATERIAL:
Three feet of soft cotton rope.

EFFECT:
The performer, having coiled up a long piece of rope on his left hand, throws it out straight and in doing so causes a number of knots to appear on it.

PRESENTATION:
Begin by holding the rope in the left hand. (Figure 1)

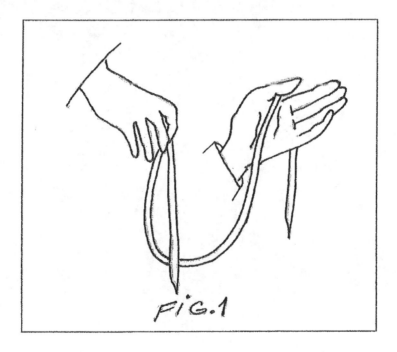

FIG.1

Pick up a piece of the rope about a yard away with the right hand, turn the hand toward you and then put the loop over the left hand. Keep on doing this until you have come to the end of the rope. Now, if you were to drop the loop from the left hand you would find that there was not a knot in the rope, but if you clip the end of the rope between two fingers and then let all the loop slide of the hand you will find that you have as many knots as there are loops.

The best way to learn this trick is to take a short piece of soft string and tie knot by passing. A loop over the hand and then passing the final end of the string through it.

Another example is to tie a knot loosely in the string and put your left hand in it; this shows you what to do if you would tie the knot magically.

Figure 2 shows some of the loops on the hand and the right hand turning the next loop inward before placing it on the left hand; furthermore, the loops should not be tight on the left hand because you want them to slide off easily.

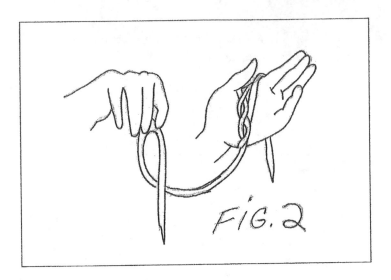

The knots appear as illustrated in Figure 3.

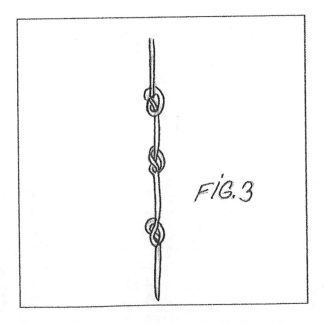

➤ THE ENCHANTED FINGER

MATERIAL:
Two feet of soft cotton rope.

EFFECT:
The performer wraps a piece of cord around the index finger of his left hand. He grabs hold of the other end with his right hand and pulls on the cord. Visibly the cord is seen to pass right through his finger.

PRESENTATION:
Pretend to grab hold of the cord with the open palm of the right hand. Instead, however, let it slide on the index finger of the right hand.
Release the index finger without pulling on the cord. Now release the little finger and ring finger. It will appear as though the cord is being held by the middle finger. Just a light tug on the cord, to release it. See steps of diagram.

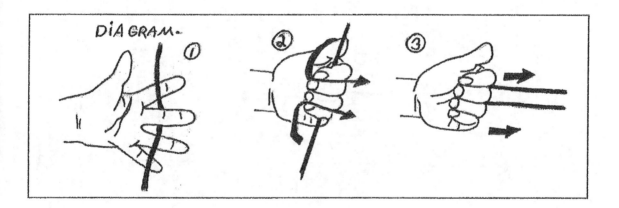

➤ STRING AND STRAW

MATERIALS:
Scissors;
One double edge razor;
One plastic straw;
White cotton string or alike (string must easily fit into straw).

EFFECT:
A common plastic straw is shown on all sides. A white cotton string is introduced and shown to be one piece. String is now lowered into the straw and is seen protruding from both sides. Straw is bent in half entrapping the string inside. The straw is cut in half and shown. The string is then pulled clear off the straw and shown to be unharmed.

PREPARATION:
Prepare your plastic straw by cutting a slit in the center about half to three quarter of an inch. (Figure 1)
For best results use a double edge razor.

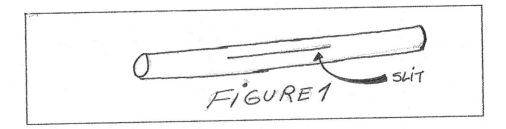

Presentation:
Show both straw and string. As you turn the straw in a rapid succession, the spectators will not see the slit. Introduce the string in the straw. Figure 2. See that it protrudes from each end.

Bend the straw at its center. Turn the straw with slit face down and bend it in half. (Figure 3)

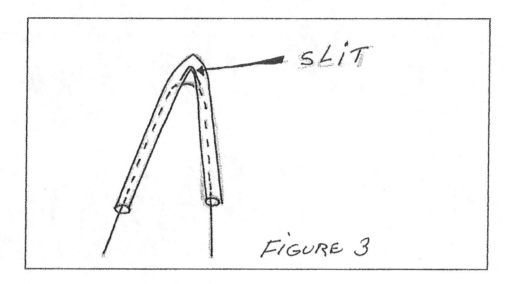

FIGURE 3

As you bend the straw tug on the ends of the string. You'll notice that the string will snap and travel to the lower portion of the slit. This is covered by your hand until such time that the straw is completely brought together. (Figure 4)

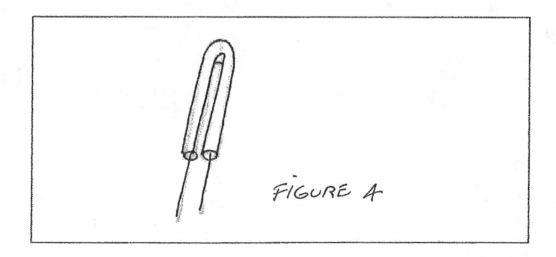

FIGURE 4

Holding the straw with one hand, the other uses the scissors to snip off the head portion of the straw. (Figure 5)

After the head of the straw has been cut, pull the string completely off and show, it in one piece.

➤ CUT AND RESTORED ROPES

An old classic but still as mysterious.
Here I give you two methods.

Method #1

MATERIAL:
3 feet of soft rope;
Scissors.

PRESENTATION:
1. Dangle about three feet of rope from left hand.
2. Run right first finger along rope and ask a spectator to say "stop" when you reach the middle.
3. When spectator says '"stop" right thumb and first finger grab hold at point a, travel back toward the left hand. (Figure 1, 2, 3, 4)

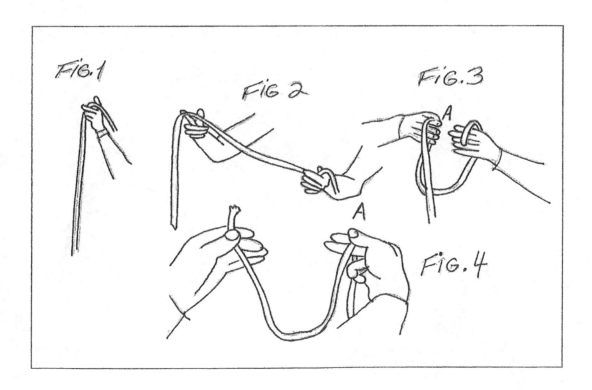

Where right first and second finger clip rope, about three inches below the end and pull it under point "A". (Figure 4, 5 and 6)

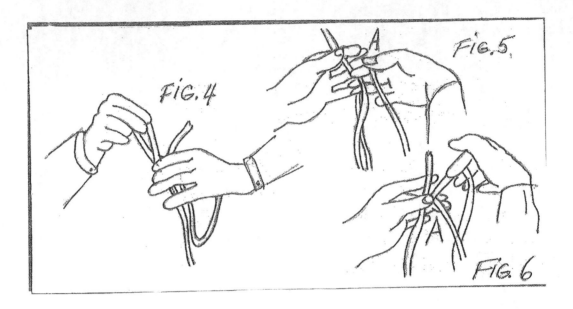

Allow the spectator to cut rope and let ends dangle, figures 7 and 8. Figure 9 shows an X-ray view of the ropes.

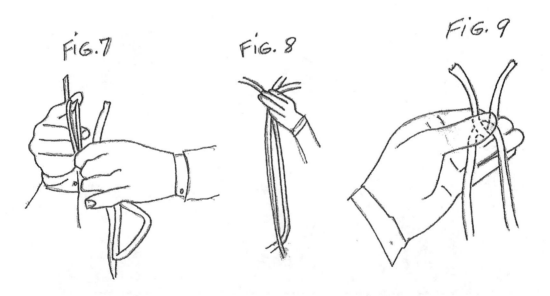

Knot these ends together and trim excess rope. (Figure 10)

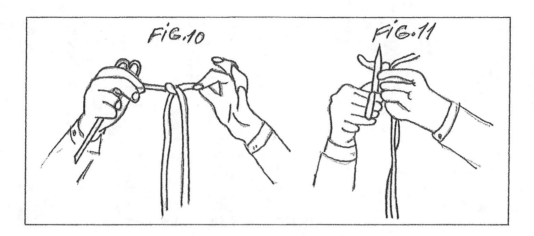

Let knotted rope dangle from left hand, and then, still holding scissors, loosely coil rope around left hand. Figure 12 and 13.

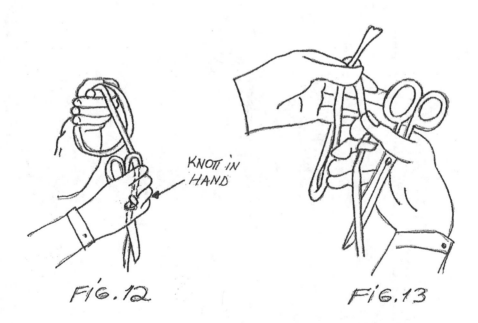

When you come to the knot- palm it in right hand and secretly slide it to the end and off the rope. The scissors help to mask this action. See figure "B".

Furthermore, it serves as a good excuse to dispose of the knot, as scissors are placed in your pocket. Grasp the end of rope, and stretch it out to show that it has been restored.

CUT AND RESTORED ROPES

Method #2

MATERIAL:
3 feet of soft rope;
Scissors.

EFFECT:
A rope is cut right through the center and restored.

PRESENTATION:
Pick up the rope, and hold it in the left hand, the end between the thumb and forefinger (this end will be referred to as A) and the other end between the tips of the forefinger and second finger (this end will be referred to as B). (Figure 1)

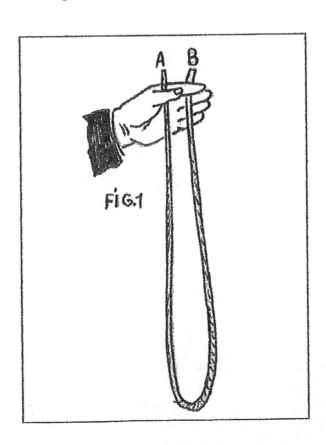

The palm of the hand is facing you. Place the four fingers of the right hand around the lower loop facing you, the hand being held below the loop. (Figure 2)

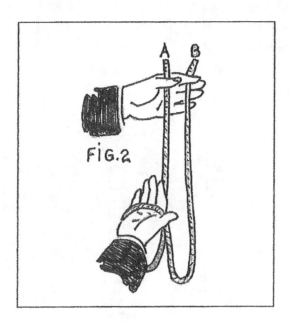

Bring this loop up, draped over the four fingers of the right hand. The right hand almost reaches the palm of the left hand, and the second and third fingers of the right hand grasp the rope seven inches below end "A". (Figure 3)

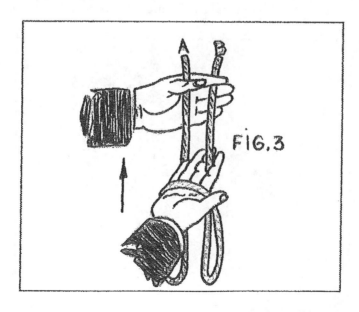

Holding the rope firmly between the second and third fingers, pull the rope through the loop, which is resting on the palm of your right hand, and continue to bring the rope up to meet your left hand. Form a loop with the rope held in your right hand, about the size of the end of the rope held in your left hand. Transfer this loop to the left hand, where it is held between the thumb and forefingers, as is end "A". (Figure 4)

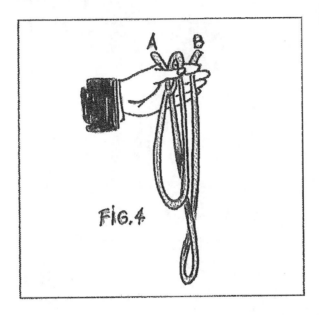

Now take the scissors in your right hand and cut through the loop held in the left hand. (Figure 5)

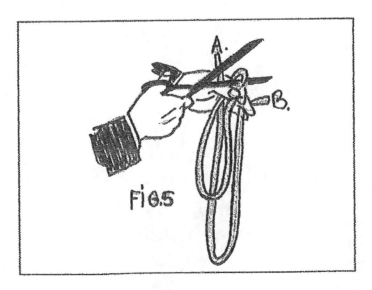

You are now holding four ends in your left hand. The end held between the thumb and the palm of the hand is end "A". There are two ends between the thumb tip and forefinger. The end nearest "A" is end "C", the end nearest "B" is end "D". You now apply pressure with the thumb and firmly hold ends "A" and "C". Allow ends "D" and "B" to fall. (Figure 6)

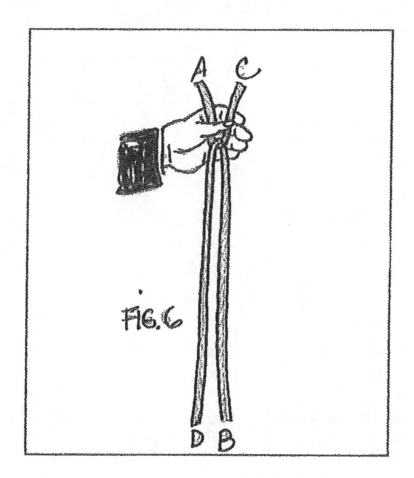

FIG.6

Tie ends "A" end "C" together with a double knot (not too tightly) and show the rope full length and tied together. Starting with either one of the two hands, the rope slides through the right hand, retain the knot in it, finally removing the knot with the right hand. You may dispose of the knot as in the previous method. Unwind the rope and show it to be restored.

ROPES THROUGH THE BODY

MATERIAL:
Two soft ropes (each about 10 feet long);
A spool of white cotton.

EFFECT:
Two ropes are wrapped around the performers waist and tied with double notes. The spectators can clearly see this and yet, as the cords are pulled by then spectators, they visually pass across his body. The ropes still bear the loops which were but a moment ago around his body.

PRESENTATION:
The ropes are prepared as in figure 1.

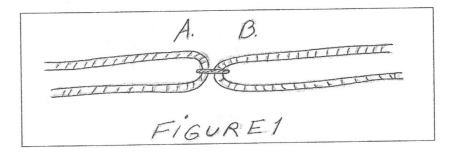

The space between the ropes have been enlarged to show how the thread is applied. In actual preparation part "A" touches part "B" which is held by the thread.
If you care to, you may show the ropes as one entire line. The connection is not noticeable. (Figure 2)

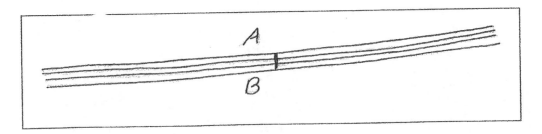

Remember to wrap the thread around A and B only once, and tie it, removing the access by snipping it off. The white thread matches color with the white ropes, therefore, its undetectable.

As you bring the ropes around your back separate them, side A from side B (see figure). Bring ropes forward to the front of your waist. Apply as many knots. (Figure 3 and 4)

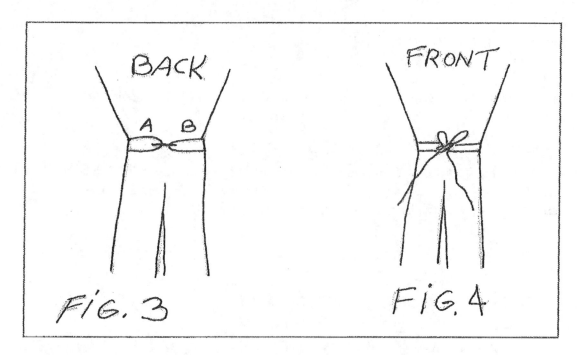

When you are ready for the release, grasp the ropes from each end and pull forward. The threat will break and the loops are spread apart. You have now passed a solid through a solid.

➤ URBUT

Method #1

MATERIAL:
A piece of string three feet long.

EFFECT:
The performer has a string cut into two, places two ends in his mouth, takes hold of the other ends, and after a bit of chewing, removes the string fully restored.

PRESENTATION:
Take a piece of about three feet long and tie the two ends together. The string is held by the four fingers of the right hand and the four fingers of the left hand. The right hand holds the knot and is facing palm upward. The left hand is facing palm downward. (Figure 1)

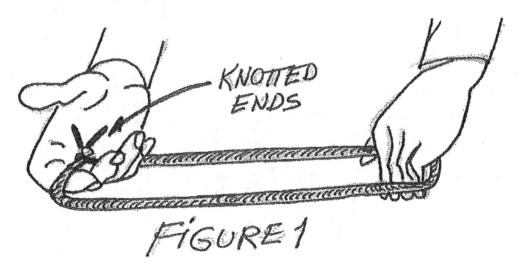

KNOTTED ENDS

FIGURE 1

You now reverse the position of the hand by turning the wrists. The right end now face palm down ward, the left palm faces upward. This movement twist the string between the hands. (Figure 2)

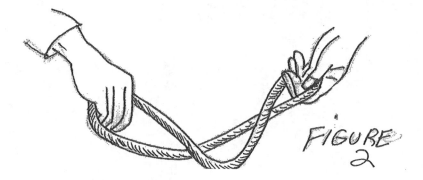

FIGURE 2

Then bring the right hand over to meet the left hand, in the above described position, and let the string fall from the right hand onto the left hand.

Immediately place the knuckles of the right hand against those of the left hand, then pull both hand apart, thus forming a double loop. This action has caused two loops to be locked together in the right hand, forming a lock. (Figure 3, as viewed by performer)

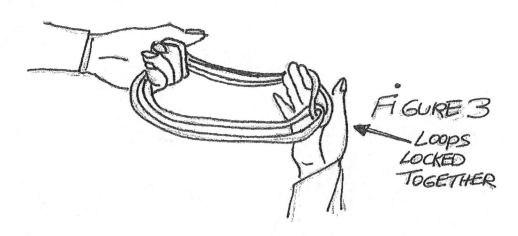

FIGURE 3
LOOPS
LOCKED
TOGETHER

Hold the string covering the "lock" between the thumb and forefinger of the right hand. With the left hand, grasp both pieces of string about an inch away from the locked position. Now ask the spectator to take the scissors and cut the two strands of string between the fingers. After the string has been cut, allow the left ends to drop, and still covering the locked position with the thumb and forefinger of your right hand, show the two pieces of string.

Place the ends and the loop held in the right hand into the mouth. Take hold of the opposite ends with each hand and go through the movement of chewing, in the meantime rnanipulating with your mouth to remove the small piece. Hide the piece under your tongue, and take the string from the mouth, showing it to be completely restored. At an opportune time take out piece from mouth and discard it.

➤ URBUT

Method #2

MATERIAL:
A piece of string two feet long (white cotton);
Scissors;
Paraffin or good bees wax.

PREPARATION:
Make an endless loop of two feet of string. The string is of white cotton and not at all heavy. The two ends of the string are fastened together with wax. Melt or soften the wax.
Cover about half inch of each end of string with wax the two ends of the string are joined and Rolled between the fingers. The ends stick together and when properly rolled, make an invisible joint. In this way a length of string becomes an endless loop. (Figure 1)

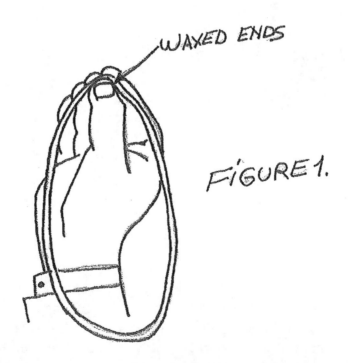

WAXED ENDS

FIGURE 1.

It is a good plan to make ten or more loops of string a one time.
Squeeze together the part of the loop which is opposite the joined ends. (Figure 2)

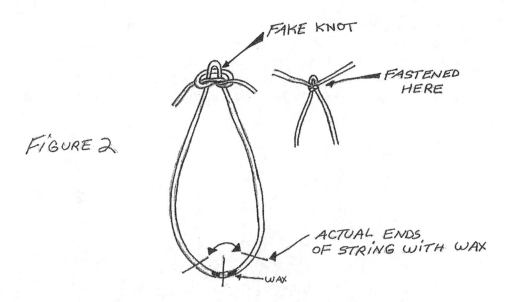

FAKE KNOT

FASTENED HERE

FIGURE 2

ACTUAL ENDS OF STRING WITH WAX

WAX

A short piece of string, the same as was used in making the loop, is now needed. Tie this short piece of string around the doubled pat1 of the loop fairly tightly and with a single knot. After making the knot, pull the loop of string through the knot until only a tiny part of the string is still inside the knot. Then cut the ends of the short piece of string leaving only about three quarter inch of string on either side of the knot. It will look exactly like a piece of string which has been made into a loop by tying the ends together. Show the loop by turning it in your hands. Take hold of the knot. (Figure 3)

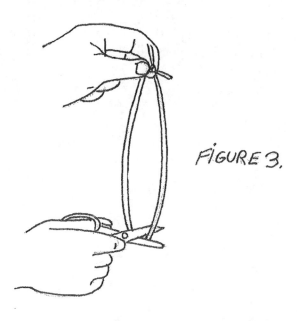

FIGURE 3.

The real ends of the string, which are waxed together, hang down. Pick up a pair of scissors and ask the spectator to watch, as you cut the string in the middle. Cut the string were it was joined by the wax. Also snip off any remaining wax from the string. See figure 2.

Purpose of course is to cut away the parts of the string which have wax on them.

Put the knot into your mouth and let the ends of the sting hang from your lips. (Figure 4)

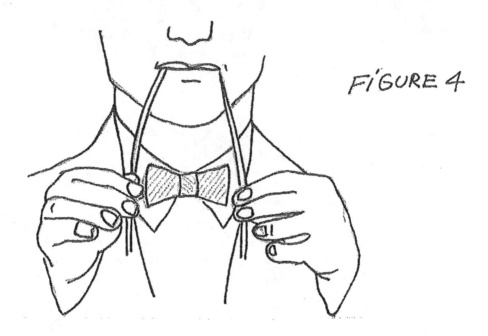

FIGURE 4

With one end of the string in each hand, pull the string out straight, and the knot pops off the string inside your mouth. With your tongue, push the knot into your cheek.

Remove it at an opportune time.

➤ RELEASE

MATERIAL:
A man's white pocket handkerchief;
A soft cotton cord 10 left long.

EFFECT:
The performer's wrists are tied with a handkerchief and the rope is made to pass through the hands and the handkerchief.

PRESENTATION:
Tell the audience that you are about to demonstrate how to pass a solid through a solid.

Place the palms of your hands together, face to face, and request a spectators to tie your wrist together with a handkerchief. Tell him to make it good and tight with a double knot. During the tying, hold your hands slightly cupped, thus obtaining the necessary slack needed for this trick. Now have the spectator insert one end of a soft rope, about ten feet long, between the arms and behind the handkerchief tying the wrist. After he has done this, he is to take both ends of the rope and stand directly front of you, as far as the rope will allow. Tell him to slacken the rope a bit so that you can move your arms up and down, and demonstrate this action.

While this action is talking place, and the rope is slackened, bring the fingers of one of the hands down between the writs, engage the loop of the rope with your fingers, pull it through and bring it over one of the hands. (Figure 1)

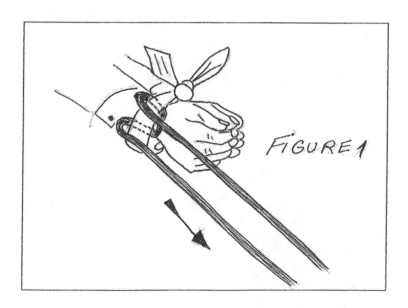

FIGURE 1

Mario Berardelli

With a bit of practice, and the proper slackness, you will find that this is not difficult at all. Of course the spectator must not see what is going on. After the above move, hold the hand steady, and out in front of you. Tell the spectator to pull on both ends of the rope, fast and hard. The rope becomes loose. The handkerchief is still tied.

➤ CUT AND RESTORED STRING

MATERIALS:
A fairly heavy pieces string;
A piece of stiff paper.

EFFECT:
A string is placed length wise in a piece of paper. String and paper are cut in half, yet, the string remains unharmed.

PRESENTATION:
Fold a piece of stiff paper with two fold and lay the string in it. (Figure 1)

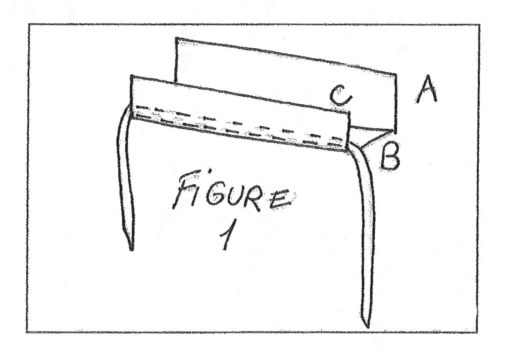

FIGURE 1

Fold over the wider side of the paper, and then fold the narrower side over this.
However, as you fold the narrower side, with the tip of the thumb push the center of the string out over the wider side. (Figure 2)

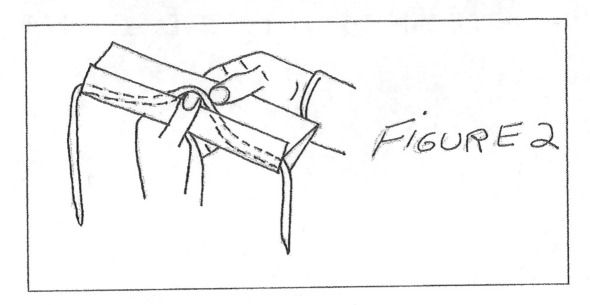

This move should not be seen by the spectators. Hold the entire assembly, as shown in Figure 3, thumb side towards yourself.

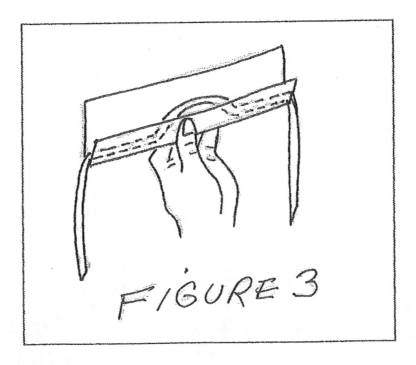

Proceed to cut, as shown in Figure 4.

What occurs is obvious. After the cut, allow the two pieces of paper to fall to the floor, revealing that the string is still in act.

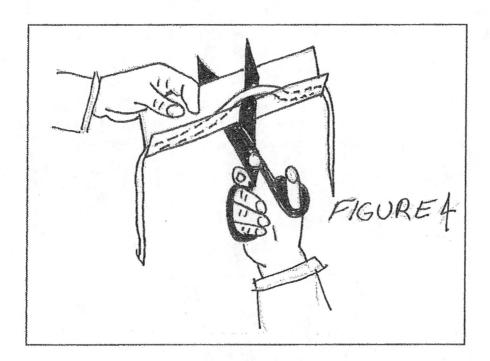

ROPE AND BRACELET

MATERIAL:
One bangle bracelet;
Four feet of soft cotton rope;
One handkerchief.

EFFECT:
A bangle bracelet is securely tied by a rope and freely shown to a spectator. The spectator holds the end of the rope, letting the bracelet bangle from the end. You have to cover the bracelet with a handkerchief and a whisk: the bracelet is shown to be free from the rope.

PRESENTATION:
Hand to the spectator the rope, the bracelet and the handkerchief for examination. Take back the rope and the bracelet and proceed to tie it as in Figure 1.

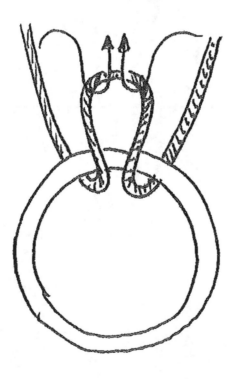

FIG. 1

Show the bracelet firmly tied by the rope. It should look like Figure 2.

FIG. 2

Instruct the spectator to hold the rope by its ends, while letting the bracelet hang free. Cover the bracelet and part of the rope with the handkerchief as in Figure 3.

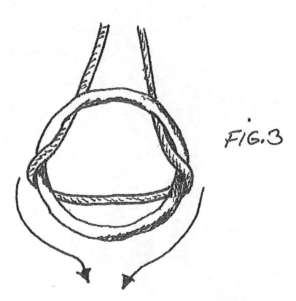

FIG.3

While the spectator is holding on, reach under cover of the handkerchief and free the bracelet.

The trick is conditioned upon the type of knot. Carefully observe figures "A", "B", and "C". Slacken the knot and pass the rope over the bracelet. the faster you do this, the better it looks. Practice it a few times to get the feel for the release. By reversing this procedure, the bracelet can be quickly tied to the rope.

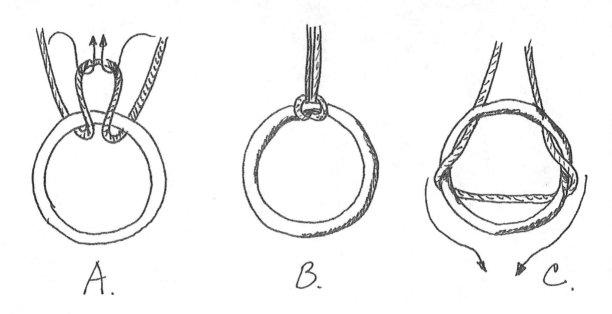

A.   B.   C.

SELF-RESTORING RIBBON

MATERIAL:
Scissors;
Pencil;
Thin strip of ribbon thirty inches long.

EFFECT:
Two ribbon are tied securely around a pencil. The ribbons are then cut in half and restored to one long strip.

PRESENTATION:
Show a ribbon approximately thirty inches long, and cut it so to form two pieces of equal length. Ask a spectator to hold an ordinary wooden pencil in a horizontal position. Grasping it at the eraser end, place the two ribbons over the pencil, as shown in Figure 1.

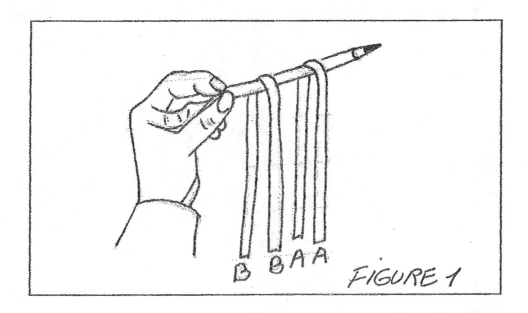

FIGURE 1

Ordinarily in tying the ribbon around the pencil, you would grasp one end of ribbon "A" and one end of ribbon "B" in one hand, and the other two ends in the other hand. Instead, grasp both ends of ribbon "A" in one hand, and both ends of ribbon "B" in the other. Tie them around the pencil, to form an ordinary knot, as shown in Figure 2.

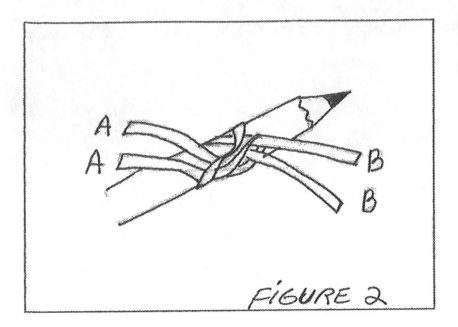

Cut the ribbons at one side, near the pencil. (in Figure 3 you see both ends of ribbon "A" being cut)

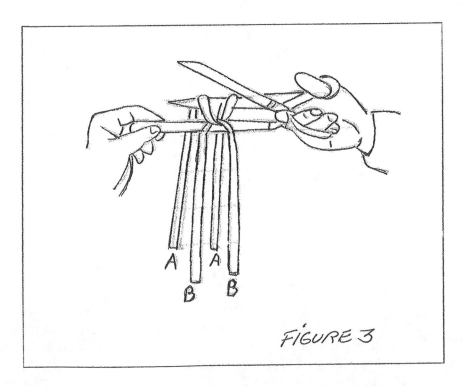

With one hand, cover the ribbons were they go around the pencil and pull the ribbons dear off the pencil. Hold the ribbons so that your thumb covers the point where the two ribbons meet. To the spectators it appears that you are holding two pieces of ribbon of equal length.
In realty, you have one long and one short piece of ribbon. (Figure 4)

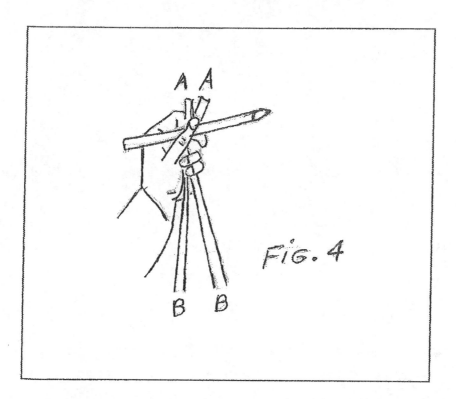

Set fire to ribbon "A". After a time, blow the fire out. Then, as a sure fire extinguisher, tap the sparks with a pocket handkerchief and carry them inside the folds of the cloth, which you deposit in your pocket. Next, grasp one end of ribbon "B" with your free hand and draw it up so that it rises vertically out of the hand holding the ribbon. Stretching the ribbon taut, pull it straight up out of the lower hand, showing the ribbon to be completely restored.

CAPERS WITH PAPERS

➤ IT'S IN THE ASHES

MATERIAL:
One pack of cigarette papers;
Rubber cement;
An ash tray or saucer;
A pencil stub;
A book of matches.

EFFECT:
A sheet of cigarette paper is torn into 8 pieces and restored. A spectator is asked to initial the restored pieces, which are placed in an ashtray and set aflame. The charred amber's are restored and the spectators signature confirmed.

PREPARATION:
Place a dab of rubber cement on corner of a pack of cigarette papers. Allow to dry. Ball up one sheet of paper and press on to corner of pack. Place in the right jacket pocket along with a pencil stub and a book of matches.

PRESENTATION:

1. Remove pack from pocket along with matches and pencil stub, securing balled paper between right first and second fingers as you do so.
2. Place pack of paper on table and open it with left hand.
3. Roll ball between tips of right thumb and right first finger and remove paper. Roll ball between right first and right second finger and tear paper in half
4. Place left piece in front of right.
5. Tear into quarters and place left pieces in front of right.
6. Tear into eight and place left pieces in front of right. Now ball up pieces and squeeze into tight ball.
7. During process switch position of balls and have finger over them. Grasp corner and pull out.
8. Roll torn ban back between right first and second finger and finish opening paper.
9. Roll ball back between right thumb and right first finger and hold restored paper by tip. Place on table and have someone initial paper.
10. Roll up paper and switch for torn pieces exactly as you did above.

11. Pull out the paper, being careful not to expose torn pieces and ask someone to strike a match for you.

12. Drop paper on ashtray and place burning match alongside it or paper will not flame away.

FINISH:

Rub tips of right thumb and right 1irst finger in ashes and slowly open paper and show initials to spectator.

THE LOOPER

MATERIAL:
A piece of cloth (can be colored) about four inches wide and about thirty inches long;
Good glue (for clothes).

EFFECT:
A band of cloth is torn into separate bands. One of these bands is again torn in the same way, but the result is two bands linked together. The second band is then torn like the first but the result this time is one long band.

Presentation:
Take the cloth and cut a slit along the middle, about one inch long. At the other end cut another slit, also along the middle, and about two or three inches long. (Figure 1)

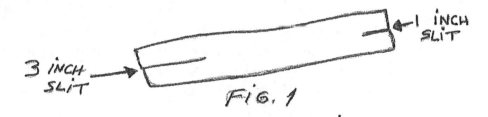

FIG. 1

Bring the two ends together, forming a band. Using the longer fanned by the longer slit, give one of them a half twist and glue it to its mate at the other end of the band. (Figure 2)

FIG. 2

Give the other longer flap a full twist, and glue this to its mate at the other end of the band. (Figure 3)

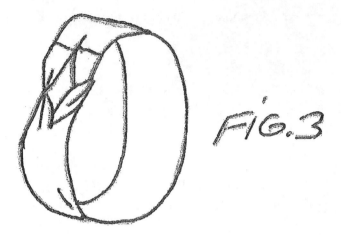

FIG. 3

When the glue has dried, flatten the prepared side so that it does not curl too much.
Hold the band so that the prepared side is toward you most of the time. Also, keep it in motion. This must be done so that the audience will have less chance to see anything on the band. Tear the band in two. (Figure 4)

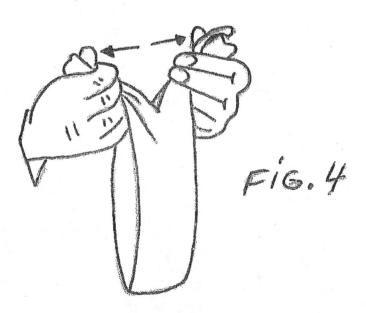

FIG. 4

Show the two bands and place the one with the half twist over your arm. Proceed to tear the other band. (Figure 5)

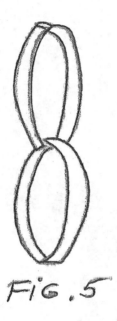

FIG. 5

You may throw out to the audience and proceed to tear the other band, and you now end up with a single band. (Figure 6)

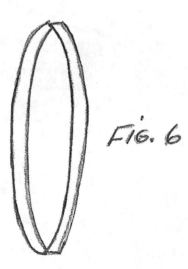

FIG. 6

Show the single, but larger band and throw this out to the spectators.

CLIP IT

MATERIAL:
A newspaper;
Scissors:
Rubber cement;
Talcum powder.

EFFECT:
A piece of newspaper is folded and then cut in two. When unfolded, the paper is seen to be restored.

PREPARATION:
Cut a column of a newspaper, about two feet long. Coat one side of this with rubber cement, allow to dry. Sprinkle this with talcum powder, it eliminates any gloss that way be seen. Remove any access by smoothing over with your fingers.

PRESENTATION:
Fold the strip of paper into two equal lengths, making sure that the prepared sides are inside the fold. With a pair of scissors cut the folded end off, cutting the strip into two pieces. (Figure l)

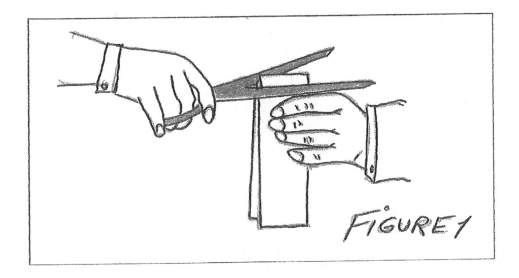

Grasp one of the uncut ends, and allowing the strip to unfold, show the spectators that it is not really cut at all. (Figure 2)

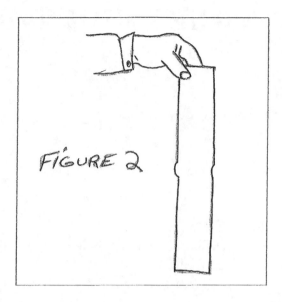

FIGURE 2

Now told the strip again (at the cut edges), but this time fold it the opposite way, bringing the prepared surface to the outside. Give the scissors to a spectator and tell him to the cut the strip. (Being careful to cut only a small portion). This is only to prove that the strip is unprepared. After the spectator has cut the strip, separate the two pieces to show that they have actually been cut, and that the restorative power is absent. Place two pieces together, prepared sides on the inside, and cut it yourself again. Proceeding as above, you then show that you have restored the strip. You may repeat this as long as you wish. As an added eye-catcher cut it in a 45° angle, Figure 3.

Open it, and watch the eyes of your spectators.

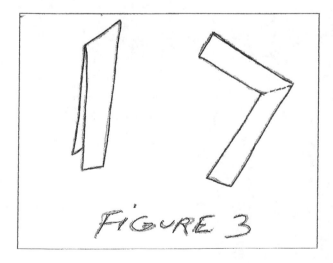

FIGURE 3

CHRISTMAS TREE

MATERIAL:
One full newspaper;
A good sharpened scissors (or you may use your hands).

EFFECT:
A newspaper (tabloid size) is rolled into a tube. It is then torn in a special way and pulled to form a very tall tree.

PREPARATION & PRESENTATION:
Roll a spread-out double sheet of newspaper (tabloid size) into a tube, allowing one end to extend freely for about three to four inches. (Figure 1)
Place the end of a second sheet on this free end Figure 2 and keep rolling, until again about three or four inches of an end remain.

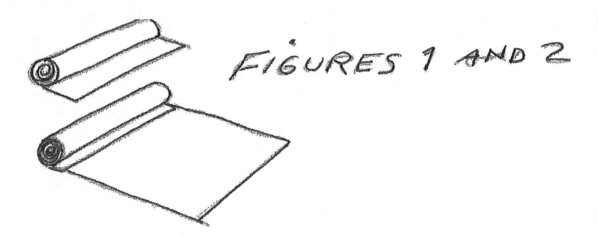

FIGURES 1 AND 2

Repeat this process with about eight to ten sheets, until you have a pretty thick tube of paper. Flatten one end of the tube and tear twice, making four separate tears, as shown by dotted lines in Figure 3.

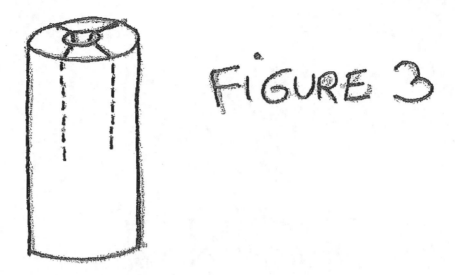

FIGURE 3

Make the tears down to about the middle of the tube. Separate the torn portions and flatten them down alongside the remaining portion of the tube. (Figure 4)

FIGURE 4

Holding the unton1 p0ltion of the tube in the left hand, insert the index finger of the right hand into the opening, and pull the inside of the up and out. Keep pulling, you will obtains tree as long as teen feet. (Figure 5)

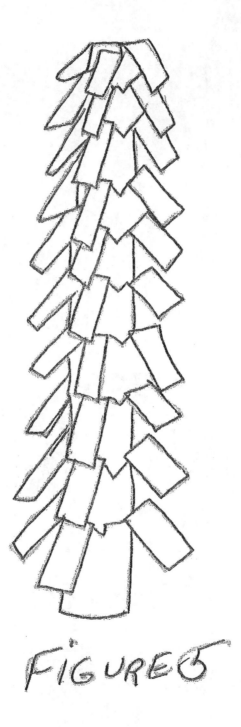

FIGURE 5

➤ TORN AND RESTORED PAPER

MATERIAL:
Two identical strips of "thin" paper, three and a half by fifteen inches;
One black magic marker (chisel point).

EFFECT:
A strip of paper with writing on it is torn to pieces and then restored immediately.

PREPARATION:
Print any identical characters on two strips of thin paper of the same size. Be sure they are exactly alike. They may be anything: A funny picture, foreign lettering, your name, or anything to which you can fit an appropriate story line. When completed, all should be identical Take one of the strips and fold it along its length like an accordion. This will give you a small thin packet. Straighten out the bottom-most pleat, Figure 1.

FIG. 1

Place some paste in the middle of the second pleat, and glue this on to the back and to the right of the second strip of paper. Glue this part about two inches from the end same distance from the long sides, Figure 2.

FIG. 2

Wait for the glue to set, fold the free pleat over the packet. Fold the upper part of the packet down, and then fold the lower part upward. (Figure 3)

FIG. 3

PRESENTATION:

Pick up unfolded strip, thumb in the rear and the four fingers in the front. Thus covering the packet from view. Be sure to have the printed characters towards the audience. Show strip this way and begin to tear the paper. You may choose to tear down the middle first. Put the pieces together so that the packet is always in the rear. Keep tearing until you have several square pieces in your hand. Fold these pieces together, toward the audience, into a small square packet. Wave your hands up and down, and during this action reverse the entire package so that the torn pieces are facing you and the un-torn strip is facing the audience.

Unfold the packet facing the audience, always keeping the packet of torn pieces toward you. When the strip is fully extended, the audience will not see the torn pieces, that are held in place in back with the thumb. You have now restored the torn pieces.

In gluing the folded strip on the back of the duplicate strip, the lettering should be inverted as compared to the other strip.

➤ EXTRAORDINARY RESTORATION

MATERIAL:
Two identical sheets of a newspaper.

EFFECT:
The performer shows a full page of a newspaper.
He asks the spectators to remember any particulars and then proceeds to tear this newspaper in many pieces. In an instant, the same newspaper is restored as before.

HOW IT WORKS:
Apply some household glue or rubber cement on the inside of newspaper "A" at the point marked with an "X". (Figure 1)

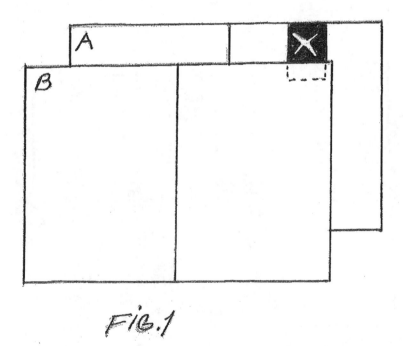

FIG.1

Stretch out newspaper "B" on top of "A" press firmly on point "X". Be sure both newspapers are properly glued and aligned. Now fold the left page "B" towards the right. (Figure 2)

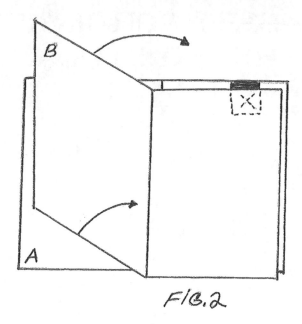

FIG.2

Fold up the lower part of newspaper "B". (Figure 3)

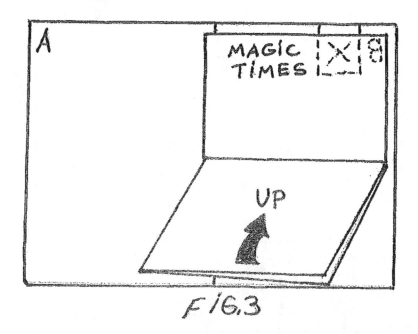

FIG.3

Continue folding newspaper B as shown until you reach a small packet. (Figure 4)

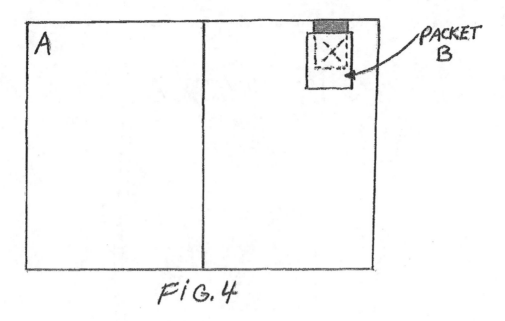

FIG. 4

Open newspaper "A", keeping packet "B" well hidden from view. Tear in half the newspaper "A". (Figure 5)

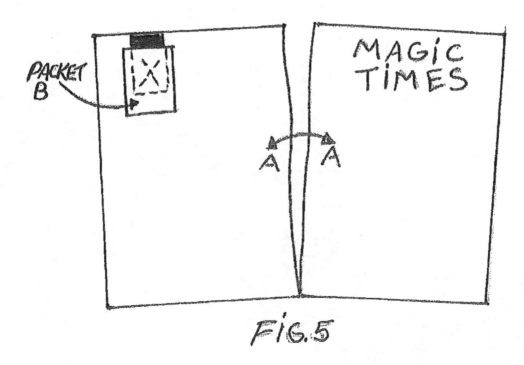

FIG. 5

Place the torn pages of A, one on top of the other. Rip these pages horizontally. (Figure 6)

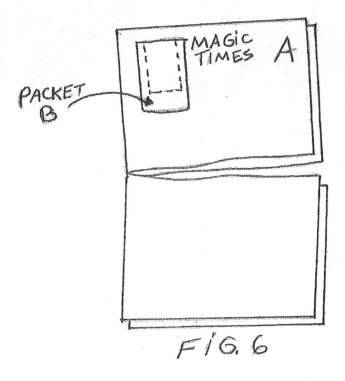

FIG. 6

Continue tearing until all the pieces of "A" are on top of packet "B" and of equal format. (Figure 7 and 8)

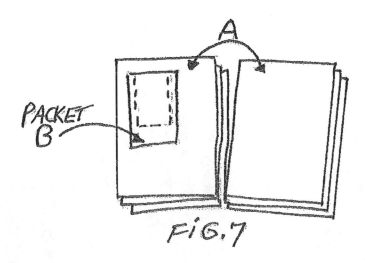

FIG. 7

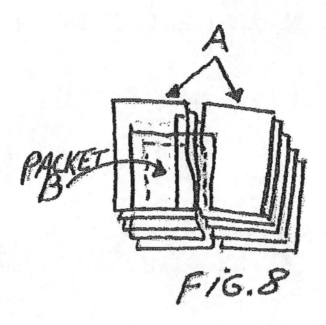

FIG. 8

Now open packet "B" little at a time. Showing the restored newspaper. Be sure to keep the torn pieces in back and well hidden. Figure 9 shows completion.

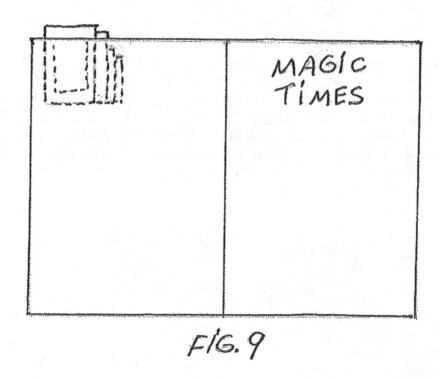

MAGIC TIMES

FIG. 9

IMPOSSIBLE EXPLANATION

MATERIAL:
Five paper napkins. If possible, eight or nine inches square.

EFFECT:
A paper napkin is torn to pieces and then restored. The trick is repeated, explaining how it was accomplished. However, the spectators become even more baffled.

PREPARATION:
Roll one of the napkins into a ball, and roll another one over the outside of it. Roll two more napkins in the same manner.
Place both napkins, thus prepared, in your right-hand pocket. Take the remaining napkin, roll into a ball, and place it into your left-hand pocket. You are now set to begin.

PRESENTATION:
Remove one of the sets of napkins from your right-hand pocket and unroll it to show an ordinary paper napkin. As you do this, you'll. Find that the inner ball will roll into your right hand, without being seen. This movement is hidden by the opened napkin.
Tear the napkin into several pieces, but always leave some sections in the right hand, thus covering the ball.
Next, roll the torn pieces inside the piece in your right and so that the ball of the torn pieces lies next to the other ball in your hand. If you care to, hold both balls together, side by side, they'll appear as one. This must be done quickly and deliberately. As you do this, rol1 the two balls so that the un-torn napkin is nearest your fingertips.
Open it in such a way so as to conceal the ball from view. Show the napkin, thus restored.
Roll this napkin into a ball, enclosing the torn papers inside it, and place ball into your right-hand pocket.

INNER
BALL

Volunteer to show how the trick was done, and explain how the two napkins are used.

Remove the single napkin from your left pocket, open it, show it to the audience and reroll it into a ball. Hold this in your right hand. Remove the balled napkins from your right hand pocket; open the outer napkin, and allow the one inside to remain in your right hand. Press the two rolled-up napkins which you have in your right hand and show them as one. To your audience it appears to be the napkin which you showed and rolled into a ball. Explain that this extra napkin is never seen, for it is hidden by the open one, and demonstrate how a napkin can be hidden behind the open one. Proceed to show how the open napkin is torn and rolled up. Show how to switch this ball for another one. Open one of the other napkins and show it restored.

Ball up this napkin and be sure to ball it around the pieces of the torn one. Place this into your pocket. One ball of paper remains in your hand. Everyone believes it to be composed of torn papers, but it is really the whole napkin. Tell your audience that if anyone should care to see this napkin all that remains is to show it. Open this napkin and take your wow's.

THE AVID PAPERS

MATERIAL:
Two types of paper can be used:

- ➤ Tissue paper of a dark color;
- ➤ Paper of fairly heavy stock. Dark in color.

EFFECT:
Three sheets of paper are shown to the spectator. Each of different color and size. The largest piece of paper is at the bottom and the smallest on top. The papers and put together and laid on table. A dollar bill is borrowed from the spectator. The bill is folded twice and placed in the center of the smallest paper. All three papers are now folded around the bill. When papers are unfolded, the bill is gone and in its place is a similarly folded piece of white paper.

Preparation:
The papers used should be different colors; "None should be white". The largest paper is 8x10 inches. The second paper is 1 inch smaller each way, that is, 7x9 inches. The smallest paper is again 1 inch smaller each way, and measures 6x8 inches. The "darkest" color paper should be used for the middle sheet, which measures 7x9 inches. The trick requires two identical sheets of this color, and a duplicate of the smallest paper.

Each paper has to be folded very carefully and exactly. Be sure that the creases are well set. Figure 1 shows where each fold is made on the largest sheet.

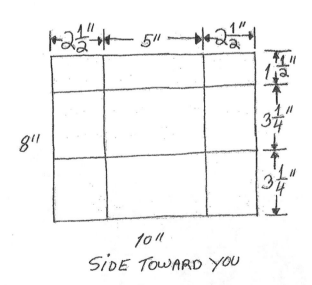

124

The inner sheets are folded with the same kind or folds the outside one has but each fold measures less. The duplicate middle sheet must be folded exactly alike. The success of this trick depends upon these two sheets being exactly alike.

Those two papers are pasted together, in their folded state, and must appear "as one" folded piece of paper. The long fold of each paper must point in the opposite direction when the paper are pasted together.

With the other hand the largest sheet is picked up and shown. All three sheets re replaced in a pile on the table. (Figure 2)

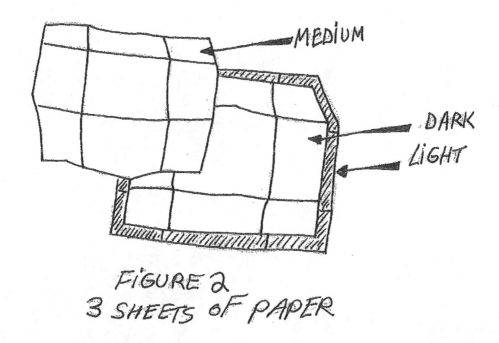

FIGURE 2
3 SHEETS OF PAPER

Borrow a dollar bill and fold it lengthwise twice. Place bill on the smallest paper and the sides of paper are folded toward the center.

Make the short front fold "the one toward the audience". Take hold of the front of this paper and fold it back onto the wide fold. Normally, the wide fold is over the paper rather than putting the paper over the wide fold.

(Figure 3, A and B)

While this is an unusual way to fold the paper it does not seem to be noticed.

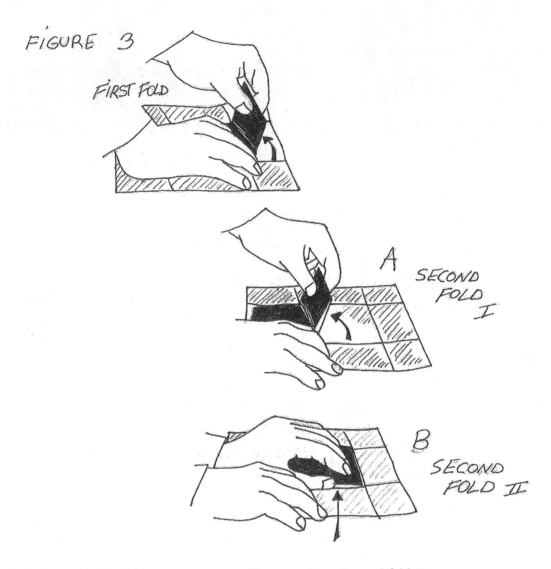

FIGURE 3

FIRST FOLD

A SECOND FOLD I

B SECOND FOLD II

As fold is being made slide paper to center of bottom sheet. Second fold II.

Prior to the trick, prepare the papers by putting onto one of the two smallest colored paper a piece of plain white paper the size of a dollar bill. This white paper has been folded twice so it is one quarter of its length. The colored paper is folded around the folded colored paper is put into one side of second colored paper. This side is folded completely and placed, face down, on the largest colored paper which has been opened out flat. The middle paper is opened out flat. That is, the upper duplicate paper is unfolded. The smallest paper is opened flat and placed on top of the pile. The long fold of the paper is toward you and in the same direction. See Figure 1.

PRESENTATION:

Begin by showing the three colored papers, lying open in a pile on the table. Show each paper separately, by raising the center edge of the nearest smallest paper until the flat surface is toward the spectator. At the same time the surface of the second can be seen. Put the smallest paper back on the second sheet, the two papers are picked up together.

This paper folded around the dollar bill is then enclosed in the second paper in exactly the same order and in the same way. In turning the paper, in the last move, onto the wide fold, the duplicate second paper is brought face up.

Finally, the biggest paper is folded around the packet. The last fold is made by bringing the wide fold onto the packet. Leave the papers on the table until the end of the trick. As each paper is now unfolded, the piece of white paper is found in place of the dollar. Reverse the process to bring back the dollar.

MENTAL MYSTERIES

X-RAY ENVELOPE

MATERIAL:
A small brown envelope;
A small sheet of square paper:
A pencil;
A lighter;
An ashtray.

EFFECT:
Someone writes a number or a name on a slip of paper. This slip is put into an envelope and burned. You look into the ashes and reveal the content.

PREPARATION:
Cut a horizontal slit across the back of the envelope, just about the center. Do not go all the way across the envelope. See Figure 1. Make sure no one sees you.

PRESENTATION:
Ask someone to write a name or a number on the slip of paper and to fold it. Raise the envelope with its open tongue in front of your friends. Insert the slip of paper inside the envelope. They will not see the secret slit which is facing you. As you insert the slip of paper make sure you slip it through the opening slit making it protrude halfway. Stop here. Raise the envelope holding with the thumb on the back, see figure. Raise it by the light and show that the slip of paper is still there. As you lower the parcel by the ash tray to light it, slip the piece of paper lower to be able to read the content. Proceed to burn it and looking into the ashes and reveal the content.

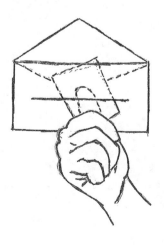

➤ TOTAL PREMONITION

MATERIAL:
A block notes 4" x 31/4" (with spiral);
A pencil;
A white chalk;
Two small slates (one slate for yourself).

EFFECT:
Four spectators are asked one by one to write a 3 digit number upon a block notice. A fourth spectator is asked to draw a line and write the total below. This spectator is given a small slate were upon hi is to write the same total in chalk. By sheer premonition you are able to give the total.

PREPARATION:
On one page of the block notice write a sequence of four numbers with three figures.
Apply a small dot besides each one and draw a line below it. (Figure 1)

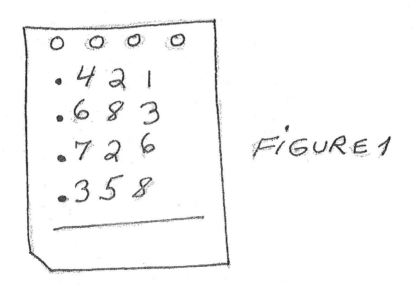

FIGURE 1

The figures must be written in different calligraphy. Leave blank the space for the total.
Take your slate and with a pencil write the total in the corner. In a way only visible to you.
Turn over the block notice and re-open it to the first page. Prepare this page by placing four dots below" each other as you've done previously. (Figure 2)

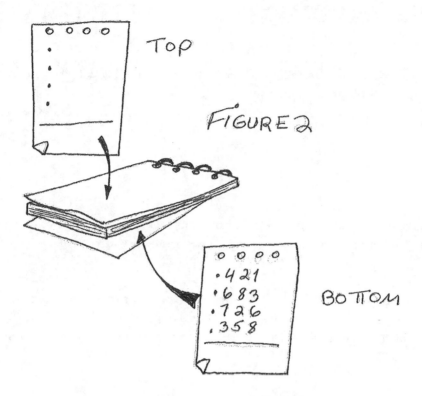

TOP

FIGURE 2

BOTTOM

. 4 2 1
. 6 8 3
. 7 2 6
. 3 5 8

Each spectator is to write the numbers besides each dot.

Have the other slate, pencil and chalk ready.

Give the block notice to the first spectator and have him write the number besides the dot. Have the other three spectators do same. The last spectator is to close the block notice and return it to you. Turn to another spectator and hand him the block notice will suspect the change. Have him sum the total and write it below the line. This will be the total which is known to you. Keep the slate with the secret total and give the other to the spectator. Instruct the spectator to write in the total in big numbers, you do the same.

Both of you now turn over the slates and match your total. It's a premonition.

➤ SWEET TELEPATHY

The following explanation may seem long. Be patient: it's sure fire. Here, I give you the most popular mind reading symbols of magic, with a sweet presentation.

MATERIAL:
Sugar cubes;
A pencil.

EFFECT:
Have a spectator mentally selects two designs from four that are drawn on two cubes of sugar. You concentrate a moment and tell the spectator what designs he is thinking of.

PRESENTATION:
Take two cubes of sugar and draw the following marks with a pencil. On one of the wide surface of the cube, draw a cross (x). On the opposite side of the sugar cube draw a circle (○). Now, on the second cube of sugar, draw a square (□) on one side and a triangle (Δ) on the opposite side. (Figures l, 2, 3 and 4)

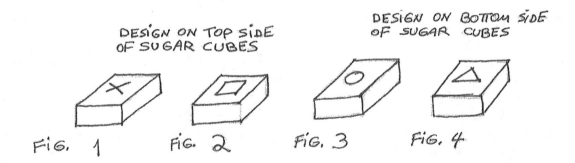

Tell your spectator that with these sugar cubes thus marked, you will try an experiment in telepathy. Turn your back, and instruct a spectator to do as follows; stack the two cubes together(one on top of the other), in the meantime making a mental note of the sugar cubes under the table in the same stacked position. You now moisten the tip of your thumb and forefinger with your lips.
Turn back to face spectators. Reach under the table with your right hand. Ask the spectator to permit you to take the sugar cubes for a moment. While you are holding the sugar cubes, press heavily with the thumb and forefingers; this action creates a pencil imprint on the sugar cubes to the spectator by dropping them into his hand. Ask him to concentrate on the two designs he noted mentally at the start of experiment.

134

While these instructions are being given, withdraw your right hand from under the table and get a glimpse or the imprints on your thumb and forefinger. (Figure 5)

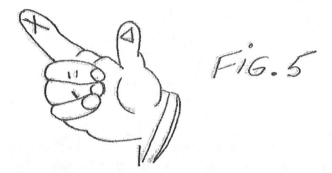

These two designs imprinted there were make from the two outer surface of the sugar cubes. The spectators is concentrating on the two designs on the inner surface of the sugar cubes. Therefore, the designs the spectator is concentrating on. You then rub your right thumb and forefinger together and the imprints will disappear, leaving no trace as to how the trick was done. These two designs imprinted there were make from the two outer surface of the sugar cubes. The spectators is concentrating on the two designs on the inner surface of the sugar cubes. Therefore, the designs the spectator is concentrating on. You then rub your right thumb and forefinger together and the imprints will disappear, leaving no trace as to how the trick was done.

➤ FLAME PREDICTION

MATERIAL:
10 Blank index cards, (5x3) without lines if possible;
10 crayons of different color;
A lighter or matches;
One saucer" if necessary;
The juice of one lemon.

EFFECT:
You hand a number of cards, each of which is blank except for a small spot of color in one corner. As your back is turned, the spectator selects one card and with a match or lighter bums of the colored mark. Take the card and examine the flame, almost immediately announcing the color.

PREPARATION:
Take the ten blank cards and place a colored mark on one of the corners of each card. Each should be a different color. About one third of the distance up from this corner, and near the opposite corner of the same side of the card, write the name of the color in lemon juice. This can be accomplished by dipping a toothpick or alike into the lemon juice. Then begin writing on paper, as you would with a pen. Do 110t stack the cards yet, wait until the writing has dried.
On the other side of the card, exactly opposite this writing, write it again with lemon juice. Again, wait until it has dried. See figures.

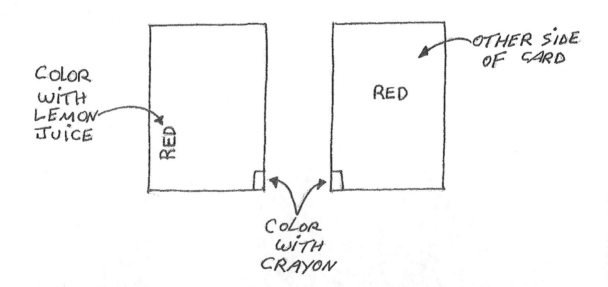

PRESENTATION:

Explain and show to the spectator that you have ten cards, each marked at the corner with a different color. Have the spectator select anyone he wishes, while your back is turned. Place your hand behind you and tell him to place the card in your hand, with the marked corner towards him. Then tell him to light the marked corner. When he is sure that the color is completely burnt off, he is to give you a signal. On average, it should not take more than a minute. Bring the card forward and act as if you are studying the flame. At the same time, casually, direct the flame towards the invisible writing. You will find that the heat of the flame makes the writing quite visible. After the card is more them halfway burnt, drop it into a saucer and announce the color.

SPECIAL NOTE:

Make sure that the interval between the time the spectator lights the card and the time you look at it is short, otherwise too much of the card will be burned. Writing on both side of the card is to prevent your having to turn the card in your hand while it is in flame.

MYSTIC PENDULUM

With this one you'll have hours of unexplained fun with your friends. It requires no manipulative dexterity on your part, and yet it always mystifies close scrutiny.

EFFECT:
A weight, tied onto the end of a string and held as a pendulum by a spectator, will respond to questions by swinging of its own in one of two different paths. A straight line or a circle.

PREPARATION:
Obtain a brightly colored stone, the size of a marble. The stranger looking the better. Tie this to one end of a string about ten inches long.

PRESENTATION:
Show the colored stone tied to the string. Have a spectator volunteer, and have him hold the end of the string with the stone hanging downward like a pendulum.
Tell him to hold it extended from his body, and as steady as possible. Request that he ask any questions that require the answer "yes" or "no". Explain that if the stone swings in the path of a straight line, the answer will be "yes". If it swings in a circular path, the answer is "no". After a moment or so, no matter how steadily the spectator tries to hold it, the stone will mysteriously begin to move- either in a straight path or a circular path. (Figure 1 and 2)

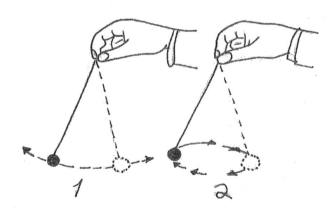

The explanation for this is rather uncertain. However, the most logical explanation is that there is a very slight muscular movement of the spectator's hand, according to whether he wishes the answer to be "yes" or "no". The spectator is completely unconscious of this action. No matter what the explanation is, it will definitely work. Try it yourself and see. You may repeat the experiment as often as you wish.

AN EXPLOSIVE PREDICTION

MATERIAL:
One dark blue balloon (not transparent);
One red balloon;
One frozen orange juice can (4 inches high with a 2 inch opening), (Color the outside of this can);
A 1/8 inch dowel sticks (Sold in 3 toot lengths);
Some strings;
One sewing pin;
Colored markers to paint the tips of the sticks.

EFFECT:
The performer begins by showing a bright blue balloon, previously blown up and secured by a string. The balloon is set aside in full view of the spectator. The performer now picks up a container which holds a number of round sticks of wood. Each one with a different color on its point. The spectator is asked to pick one at random. The blue balloon is touched with this stick, say red. There is a bang and the blue balloon changes to red, the same color found at the point of the stile.

PREPARATION:
The sticks should extend beyond the top of the container and also be easy to pick out.
The sticks should be 5 inches long. Seven such sticks can be cut from one dowel. Cutting up three dowel sticks will give of the 5-inch long sticks to do the trick. If four dowels are used in making the color sticks, the trick is even more impressive.
Every stick in the container bears the color red on its tip. Only three sticks are of a different color. To help you see this, place a black dot on top of the three sticks.

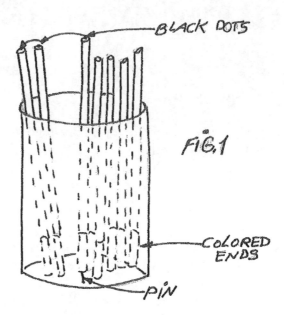

The secret of the color changing balloon is that one balloon is blown up inside another. The red balloon inside the blue one. The outer balloon has a little more air in it than the inner one. That leaves a little airspace between the two balloons.

When the pinpoint is stuck into the outer balloon it burs1s and the inner balloon is revealed. (Figure 2)

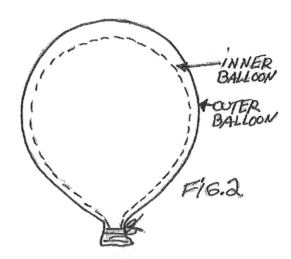

Be sure that the tube of the inner balloon is knotted with string. Then a little more air is blown into the outer balloon. Finally, put a pin in the end of one of the odd colored sticks. The hole should be

¼ inch deep into the stick and the point of the pin is cut 14 inch from its tip. Push the blunt end of the pin into the stick. (Figure 3)

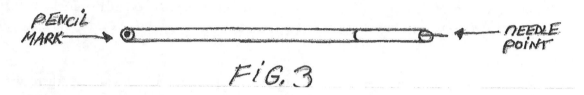

PENCIL MARK → ⟵ NEEDLE POINT

FIG. 3

PRESENTATION:

Carrying the container to one spectator, the performer asks him to mix the sticks as the performer has done. After the sticks have been mixed the performer invites the spectator to select one stick and take it out of the container, but to hold his other hand around the colored tip so no one can see the chosen color. The container, with its remaining sticks, are put back on the table.

The performer picks up the balloon with his left hand, covering the tube (opening), and with the right hand picks up one of the colored stick, with the pin.

Have spectator remove his hand from the stick, which will reveal the color '"Red". He is asked to name the color red and as he does, the performer punctures the outer balloon to reveal the red one, as the correct prediction.

LOCK AND KEY

MATERIAL:
A lock and five keys that will open it. Four keys that look just like the real ones and that fit the locks, (but do not open it). A transparent plastic bag of about a gallon size (3,7 liters) used to store food.

EFFECT:
One lock and five keys, only one key opens the lock. The right key is mixed with the others, yet you find the key that opens the lock.

SETUP:
Four of the keys that open the lock are together under the opening of the bag. The others, including one key that opens the lock, lie inside the bag. The lock is on display.

PRESENTATION:
Two people come up to assist you. They examine the locked lock. Bring forward the bag of keys. Your left hand conceals the four keys at the opening. They are just under the inside edge were you can drop them later. Drop the keys in view on the table. Keep the bag down to you side. Have each key on table tried and verified that only one opens the lock. Take only the four keys that don't work and drop them into the bag.

THE SWITCH AND SECRET:
The right hand picks up the four keys from the table. As it comes over the top of the bag held in the left hand, the right hand closes in around it's keys and the left hand opens so that the other keys drop into the plastic bag.

CONTINUE:
The keys are given a quick shake and the bag is given to one of the spectators. The last key is dropped into the bag with the others and mixed up by the other spectator. The keys are removed at a one time until you stop the process at the key that opens the lock.

SENSE OF COLOR

MATERIAL:
A good stiff cardboard;
One (new) sharpened pencil;
A tempera paint-red, green and blue.

EFFECT:
While your back is turned, one of three different color disc is placed in your hand, and by mere sense of touch you divine the color.

Preparation:
Prepare three different colored cardboard discs. They should be no more than two inches in diameter. Color them red, green and blue. Through the center of each disc punch a hole. Each of these holes must vary in size. Get a small stub of a pencil, making sure that it is well sharpened. Make the hole in the red disc so then when the point of the pencil is placed through it, only about two-thirds of the point penetrates; make the hole in the green disc so that almost the entire point penetrates; make the whole in the blue disc so that the entire pencil goes through it.
See figures 1, 2, 3.

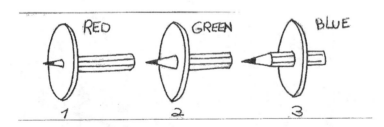

PRESENTATION:
Tell your audience that you have very sensitive fingers and that by more touch you can distinguish colors.
Hand the three disc to A spectator; turn your back to him and tell him to piece anyone of the discs in your hand. Face the spectator again, keeping the disc behind you, assume some deep concentration.
At this time, remove the pencil from your back pocket and insert the point into the hole in the disk. Depending upon how far the pencil enters, you can name the color. Hide the pencil in your back pocket so you can repeat the trick.

MIND OVER FLAME

MATERIAL:
A book of matches;
One very sharp pencil.

EFFECT:
A spectator is asked to hold a match and to light it. While he concentrates on his name, his initial mysteriously appears on the burnt-out match head.

PREPARATION:
Secretly find out the name of any spectator or friend in your group, preferably unknown to you. Print the initials, with a pencil, on the head of a paper match, still attached to the packet; use heavy strokes.

PRESENTATION:
Say. "I' am going to prove mind over matter".
Take the packet of matches out of your pocket, tear out the match with the spectator's initials on it, light it and hand it to him.
After he blows the light out, tell him to look into the head of the match, the initials of his name will be seen. Watch his surprise.

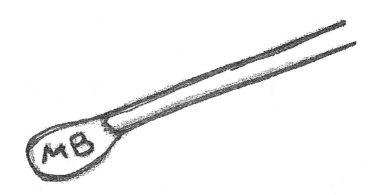

FANTASTIC STUNTS

THE WEIGHT LIFTER

EFFECT:

You ask a volunteer, who looks fairly husky and strong, to stand in front of you. You tell him that he will not be able to lift you, he tries and fails. As you now tell him he can, he'll be able to do so.

PRESENTATION:

Select a volunteer much larger and stronger than you. This experiment becomes more convincing. Have him stand in front of you. Hold your elbows to your sides, hands pointed up. Shift the elbows forward a bit. This shifts your center of gravity backward, so as to become difficult to lift you. When you ask him to lift you by your elbows, he will not be able to, or it will be hard to. Now, shift your elbows back to your sides. As you now tell him he can lift you, he can. Mind over matter.

NOTE:

Present this trick as power of suggestion.

JUST A TOUCH

EFFECT:
A volunteer sits in his chair. You merely touch him on the forehead and he is unable to stand.

PRESENTATION:
Tell your friend (audience) that you're about to demonstrate your magic powers and would like someone to volunteer for the experiment. Have your volunteer sit in a chair and tell him to relax completely. His hands should be on his lap in a relaxed position with head tilted far back as possible. When he has assumed such position, tell him not to use his hands. Tell him that you will just touch his head with your forefinger and when you do so, try as he may, he will not be able to stand. (Repeat this statement)

NOTE:
Place your finger against his forehead and tilt his head as far back as possible. Now tell him to stand. The center of gravity has been shifted. Remove your finger and tell him to stand.

MAGICAL ESCAPE

EFFECT:
Though your hands are tied and you're wearing a suit, nevertheless, you remove your shirt.

NOTE:
You must be wearing a suit, a shirt and tie.

PREPARATION:
The shirt must be put on in a special way. Throw the shirt over your shoulder like a cloack. Button the collar and the first two buttons of the shirt. Button the cuffs on the wrists. Put a tie on the vest and jacket as normal and button them.

PERFORMANCE:
Announce that you can pass a solid through a solid. Hand someone a piece of rope, long enough to tie your wrists together. Tell them to do this any way he wishes. But to make sure it is possible for you to loosen your hands in any way. Now, you must go in a closet, behind a screen or room alone. You'll find you can move your hands and wrist. Begin to loosen your tie (do not untie it) and take it off over your head. Unbutton your collar and the rest of the button in front of the shirt. Unbutton the cuffs with your teeth. It is not hard with a little practice. Take hold of the shirt collar on back and pull on it, the shirt comes off. Replace the tie on your neck as normal as before. Put the shirt over your arm and now make your presence.

SHIRTLESS

EFFECT:
After unbuttoning several buttons of your friends shirt, you take hold of the shirt collar and pull hard in an upward sweep. Magically the shirt comes off.

NOTE:
For this magical stunt you must have a (stooge) a friend of yours in the audience (group of friends) unknown to anyone there.

PREPARATION:
Ask your friend to remove his coat, then his shirt and tie. Drape the shirt over his back. Button the collar around his neck. Put tie on in a normal fashion. Bring the sleeves of the shirt down his arms and button the cuffs on the wrists. Have him replace his vest (if he has one) then his coat. Have him sit with the group of people.

PERFORMANCE:
Call for a volunteer. Your friend comes up. Say "you will perform a magical feat". Have him remove his tie and unbutton his collar: You then unbutton his cuffs. Ask if he feels more relaxed this way. He acts and thinks you are crazy. You now reach behind him and grasp the back of the shirt collar. With a sudden upward sweep, pull the shirt completely off. Tell him he should feel much more relaxed, as the audience (friends) are jumping with laughter.

PUZZLES

Here, we embark on the road of betting. Just for fun, of course. "Ever since Adam and Eve were beguiled with the famous apple trick", charlatans and tricksters have used the streets to amaze and sucker our adolescent minds. The psychology that makes this work, is not far from that of a magician. However, you may refer to some of the previous material in this book, such as, optical illusion, thirty one bet, odds or even)super Monte and heads or tails; these tricks can be used as a friendly bet for coffee or as a magical feat. The idea here, is to entertain… amaze and have fun with yourself and those around you.

This piece of history, still being used today is right in the van of carnival swindles. "The easier it looks, the harder it becomes". Forgive me if I use the word "sucker", it is not intended to insult anyone, rather implies the jargon used by charlatans.

THE CARNIVAL SPOT

WHAT HAPPENS:

The sucker is confronted by a red circular spot measuring five inches in diameter painted on the counter. He is given five flat discs each measuring slightly more than three inches in diameter. The object of the game is to cover the red spot completely using nothing more than the five discs. Figure 1 shows execution.

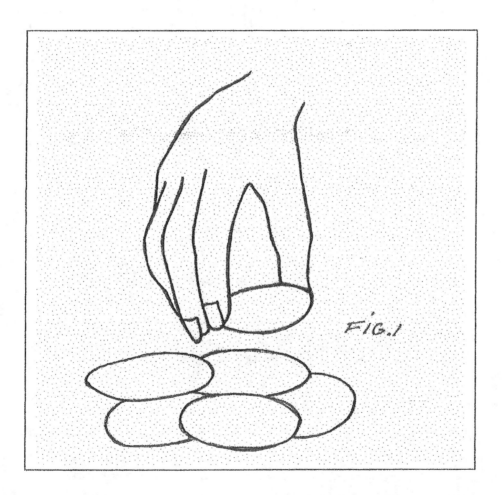

FIG. 1

Obviously the spot is the largest possible that can be legitimately covered by the discs, which must be dropped onto the spot one at a time and, once in position, cannot be moved again. The merest speck of red showing means that the game is lost. Needless to say, the sucker loses every time.

There are various methods of fleecing the public with this game. They include painting the spot on oilcloth so that its shape can be subtly distorted by stretching and using a key disc that is itself distorted.

First have the sucker drop the discs as he thinks will fit from a height of about six inches. The slightest deviation with any disc will spell failure.

A skilled player can average about one in three or two to one against. The probability that he will score five perfect drops are one in three or 243. Of course the more attempts he makes the more he'll come to reassume along exact geometrical lines.

Figure 2 shows the arrangement which most people work in their minds.

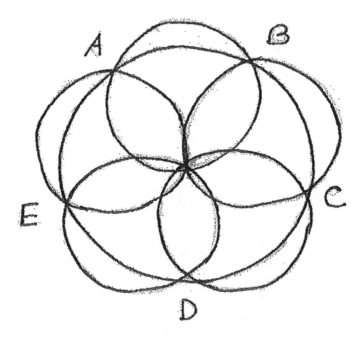

FIG. 2

Allow the sucker to place the discs down carefully without dropping them. The odds are that he will attempt to arrange them as figure one. This action only covers the center part of spot, leaving the small specs of red showing at A, B, C, D and E. Naturally, the sucker looses.

Figure 3 reveals the proper arrangement which you then proceed to show him.

FIG. III

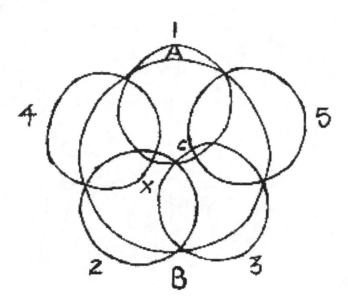

Look carefully at diameter AB. First put disc 1 into position, making sure that its center rest on AB and that the base of its circumference X is slightly below the center of the spot, C. next put down discs 2 and 3 so that their circumferences pass through X and B, where upon discs 4 and 5 fall obviously into place. The exact measurements for the spot and the discs are respectively.

The distance CX works out at about 0.07 inch. Nothing less than 3.045 will cover the 5 inch spot, as shown in the winning method. Attempting the first arrangement will result in failure. Using that method you would need discs 3.09 inches in diameter. The goal for which the operator should him is to be able to effect the second arrangement.

As rapidly as possible seemingly dropping the discs from a height of six inches, but in fact-by using the misdirection provided by swift up-and-down and back-and-f011h movement of the hand-making the drops from no more than 1 inch above the spot.

➤ UP AND DOWN

MATERIAL:
Three tumblers.

PRESENTATION:
Line up three tumblers, one open end down, one open end up, and the last open end down, see figure.

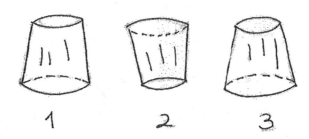

Only in "three moves", have all three tumblers open end pointing up wards on a table. During each move you must turn two tumblers over, one per each hand.
Try this one, you'll have hours of fun with your friends and family.

SECRET:
First turn over tumbles 1 and 2. Second, turn over 1 and 3 and third, turn over 1 and 2.
These moves should be done in a fluid succession, from start to finish.

➤ DIME AND TUMBLER

MATERIAL:
One dime;
Two quartos;
One tumbler

PRESENTATION:
Place a dime on a cloth covered table. Next, place a quarter on either side of the dime. (Figure 1)

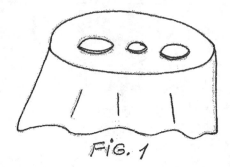

FIG. 1

The quarters should be so placed that an inverted tumbler will rest on the coins. (Figure 2)

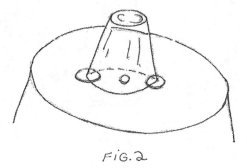

FIG. 2

PRESENTATION:
you must remove the dime from under the glass without touching the glass or the quarters.

SECRET:
Place your forefinger on the table opposite the dime, and scratch the cloth lightly, the dime will move slowly in the opposite direction. Soon it will come out under the glass.

➢ DICE CATCHER

MATERIAL:
Two dice;
One paper cup.

PREPARATION:
Pick up a paper cup with your right hand. Next, grip one die with your thumb and forefinger, and then balance a second die on top to fit. See figure.

PRESENTATION:
The object is to get both dice into the cup by tossing them in the air, one at a time. Catching the first die is easy, the second one is not, it always seems to pop out of the cup.

SECRET:
After the first die is in the cup, release the second die and quickly drop your hand, with the cup, down and under the die so that it falls into the cup.

➢ FIELD GOAL

MATERIAL:
4 ice cream sticks;
4 kitchen maturate sticks;
Any coin.

PPREPARATION:
Arrange the coin and match sticks as in Figure 1.

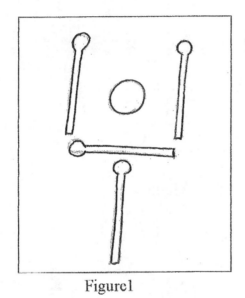

Figure1

PRESENTATION:
You must remove the coin from the field goal by moving two of the stick to new positions.

THE CATCH:
You cannot move the coin, and you must retain the exact shape of the field goal.

SECRET:
Slide the stick on the "bottom" of the goal partway to the left. Then move the stick that is on the "right" side of the goal to the left of the "stem". The goal is now upside down, and the coin is on the outside. See Figure 2.

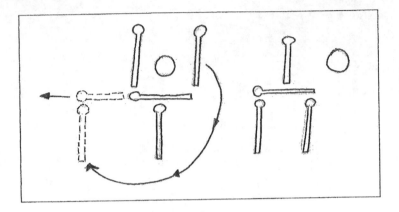

Figure 2

WHICH WAY

MATERIAL:
Two matchboxes (the kind with a label on both sides);
A razor blade.

PREPARATION:
From a matchbox remove the drawer from the sleeve and with a razor blade cut it carefully into two across its center width.

You now re-assemble the matchbox but reverse one half of the drawer in the process. If you now open the box at one end by a third it will appear the correct way up; open it from the other end and the drawer will appear upside down. Fill this zing sag drawer with matches and you are ready to amaze your spectators.

Illustration shows the way box should look.

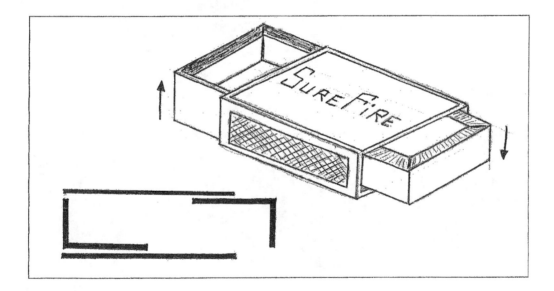

You will also need an ungimmicked matchbox of the same design. This one goes to the spectator. You retain the gimmicked box.

Ask your spectator to follow every action you do.

1. Open the box so that the matches are showing. Try to remember which end shout the matches. Make sure that the matches in both boxes lie the same way. You do not want all the striking heads at one end.

2. Close the box.
3. Turn it over sideways.
4. Turn it over length ways.
5. Again turn it over.
6. Open the box and take out a match.
7. Here is where the spectator misses. Your box is the right way up, but his is upside down, the bottom of his drawer forms a barrier between him and his matches.

➤ WALKING THROUGH A CARD

Here's one that I am sure you'11 get some funny looks from your spectator. Nonetheless, be serious on your bet, at first. The laughs come at the end.

MATERIAL:
Good sharp scissors;
A good poker size playing card.(Use a good brand);
Razor blade.

PRESENTATION:
''I'll bet you that I can cut a hole in an ordinary playing card and step right through it". "Be patient and watch me".

HERE'S HOW:
Fold the card down the middle, and with a razor cut a line in the center within a quarter of an inch of each end. (Figure 1)

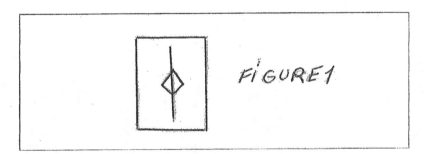

FIGURE 1

Now, with a sharp razor or scissors, cut through both thickness, once to the right and once to the left. Stop within a quarter of an inch of the edge. (Figure 2)
These cuts are about an eighth of an inch apart.

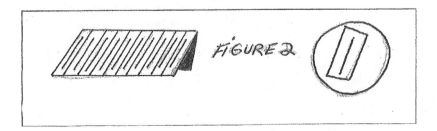

FIGURE 2

The card when opened will look like figure 3. Open it out still further and it will form an endless strip for you to step through.

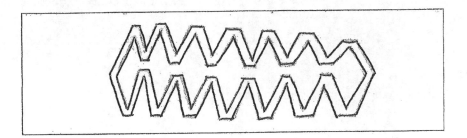

THE BLACK HOLE

MATERIAL:
Scissors;
A sheet of paper;
One quarter;
One dime;
A pencil.

PREPARATION:
Use the dime as a guide, to draw a circle onto the middle of the paper. Carefully cut this out of the paper. (Figure 1)

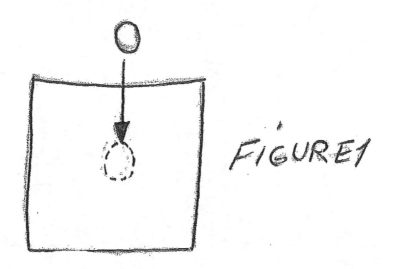

FIGURE 1

PRESENTATION:
The trick is to push the qUal1er through the hole without tearing the paper.

SECRET:
Fold the paper across the middle of the hole. (Figure 2)

Insert the qum1er inside the folds towards the opening. Pick up paper and coin as in Figure 3.

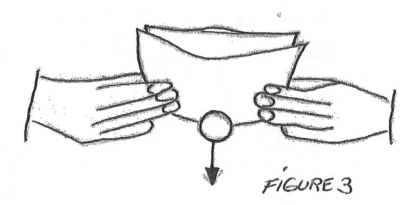

And bend the corner of the paper towards each other. The hole will enlarge, without tearing around the quarter.

➢ ALL TIED UP

MATERIAL:
2 soft cotton ropes
The lengths are not given, as you would need to experiment with it yourself.

PREPARATION:
Loosely tie a length of rope to both of your wrists. Have your friend do the same with another piece of rope that has been looped over the first rope. See figure.

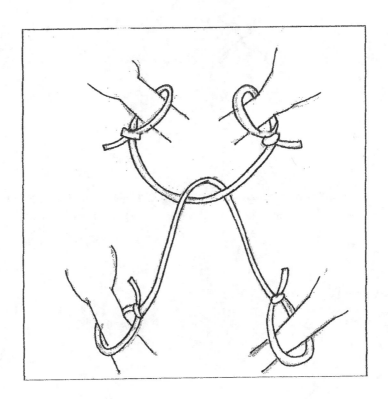

PRESENTATION:
You are to separate yourself from your friend without untying the knots cutting the ropes, or slipping your hands out of the loops.

SECRET:
Pass the loop of your rope through the loop which encircles one of your friend's wrists, slide it over the hand, and pass it back again through the loop. The ropes will now be separated.

TOOTHPICK FISH

Take eight toothpicks and arrange them as in Figure 1.

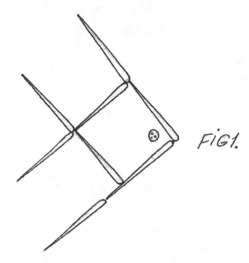

FIG1.

Place a button in the square for an eye. You must cause the fish to tun1 in the opposite direction. Explain to the spectator to move only three of the toothpicks, and the button.

SECRET:
Move the three toothpicks shown by the dotted lines of fish A. And replace them in the position indicated by the dotted lines in fish B.

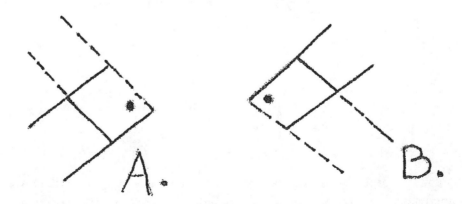

A.   B.

➤ ICE CUBE

Present this trick with an ice cube and a partially filled glass of water. Next, get a foot long piece of cotton thread or thin string.

Ask the spectator to remove the ice cube from the glass with the string without tying any knots. You cannot tie a loop in the string and you cannot touch the ice cube with your finger. He can try as much as he likes, but he will not succeed, not even by placing the string beneath the cube and attempting to balance it precariously.

SECRET:

Take the string, and soak it in the water, and then double it into a loop at the centre.

Place the loop onto the ice cube and pour salt over them both (practice will show you the right amount). Wait a bit and you will then be able to lift the ice cube with the string which will have become frozen to it. In short, the salt will cause the ice under the string to melt. In turn, as the salt water flows off the top of the cube, the water will freeze around the string, but this time with the string embedded in it.

THE WATER PITCHER

Have a water pitcher full of water and place it on your table. If at someone's house simply ask for it. Also have an empty glass tumbler and you're set to go.

Tell the spectator that he is to fill the glass tumbler with the water in the pitcher, and yet leave the pitcher with exactly the same amount of water in it as before.

SECRET:

Merely take glass and gently lower it into the pitcher until it fills with water and sinks to the bottom. The glass will now be filled, yet the pitcher will still contain the same amount of water as before.

➤ PIZZA

Try this, next time you're having pizza with your friends. It may help you to win a free slice.
A whole pizza must be divided into eight equal pieces using only three cuts with a pizza wheel. All
these cuts must be in a straight line. Give up?

HERE'S HOW:
Slide the pizza in half. Again in half, but in the other direction. You now have four quarters.
(Figure 1)

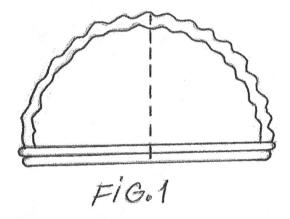

FIG. 1

Stack the four pieces on top of each other.
Cut this in half with your third cut. You now have eight pieces. (Figure 2)

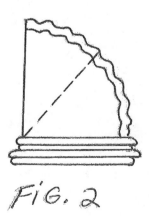

FIG. 2

A POTPOURRI OF MAGIC TRICKS

➤ ALADDIN'S BOTTLE

MATERIAL:

One small to medium glass bottle with narrow neck (For example "a dark beer bottle" may be used, it must not be transparent);
A soft cotton rope (This must fit inside the opening just so);
A small rubber ball or a piece of cork.

EFFECT:

A glass bottle is freely shown to be empty. A soft cotton cord is them introduced inside the bottle. After some magical passes the bottle is turned upside down, the rope does not fall out. Grasping the end of the rope, the bottle does not fall off.
All may be swung back and forth. At the end, the rope is removed and all shown freely.

PREPARATION:

Make a small soft rubber ball, or just make one from a piece of cork. The circumference of the ball plus the circumference of the rope you will use should be slightly larger than the neck of the bottle. When ready, place all material next to you on table.

PRESENTATION:

Briefly talk about Aladdin's bottle and the story that surrounds this mystical hire. Proceed to demonstrate. Pick up one end of rope and allow the loose end to enter the bottle. While holding the rope with the right hand, pick up the bottle with the left hand and turn over slowly, so that the bottle is upside down and rope below it. (Figure 1)

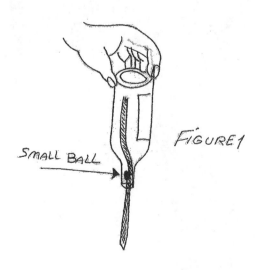

SMALL BALL   FIGURE 1

In doing this the small ball will fall against the rope at the neck of the bottle. A slight tug on the rope will carry the ball into the neck, thus holding the ball by pressure. Let go of the rope and show that it hangs freely.

Grasp the end of the rope again and allow the bottle to swing free. (Figure 2)

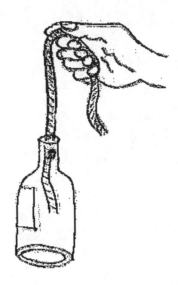

The grip between the cord and ball is tight, thus you may swing the bottle. (Figure 3)

When you have finished your demonstration, hold the bottle at the neck, Figure 4.

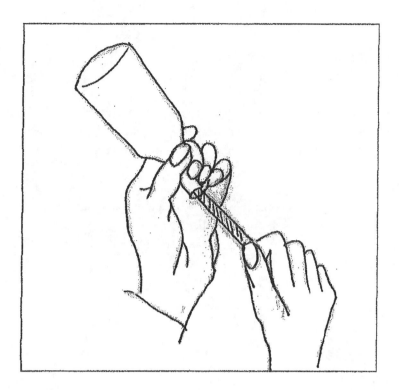

You may do two things:

-You may gently pull the rope with steady pressure. This will bring the rubber ball out of the bottle, with the rope. The ball will fall into your palm, hidden from view.

-By inverting the process, you allow the ball to fall in the bottle by pushing the rope inward. Bottle is right way up. Pull rope clear off: turn bottle over and ball will thus fall in your palm.

In this way, the ball must be a tad smaller than the neck of the bottle.

Try both methods and feel whichever is comfortable.

THE MAGIC SPOOL

MATERIAL:
One spool of cotton thread used in sewing, use 2 or 3 feet.

EFFECT:
Show the spectator a spool of sewing thread. Remove 2 to 3 feet in length. Show it to be solid. Show it to be solid, then begin to snap the thread into small pieces and gather them like a pellet. Find the leader and begin pulling, the thread is seen to be restored.

PREPARATION:
Cut off 2 or 3 feet of thread and carefully roll it into a pellet between your right thumb and first finger. Make sure to leave a tiny leader to the pellet.
Secure the pellet under the right thumb and first finger. The leader is pointing towards the thumb tip. (Figure 1 and 2)

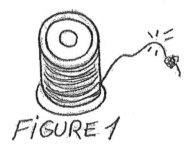

FIGURE 1

FIGURE 2

PRESENTATION:
First of all no one must know of the secret pellet under your thumb. Try to make no evidence to this fact.
Show the spool of thread and immediately remove desired amount. See preparation. With the fingers of both hands snip of small pieces, one at a time.
Do not be afraid of the secret pellet, it will not be noticed. (Figure 3)

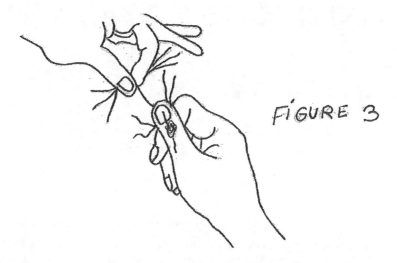

FIGURE 3

As the keep thumb and fingers of left hand close to the right fingers as they begin to roll the broken pieces.

Now, keep fingers of both hands close together. The left thumb and fingers begin to roll the broken pieces. The right thumb and first fingers must simulate the same action. Here comes a role reversal. The thumb and first finger of the left hand retain the balled and broken pieces.

The left thumb and first finger grab the lead from under the right thumb extracting the string, which is shown to be restored. (Figure 4)

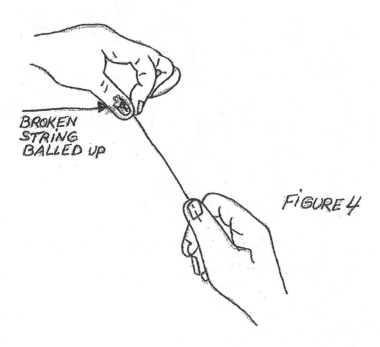

BROKEN
STRING
BALLED UP

FIGURE 4

UNLINKING SAFETY PINS

MATERIAL:
Two large "all metal" safety pins (Please try to use new pins).

EFFECT:
Two ordinary safety pins are linked together by a spectator. You are able to unlink these by pulling them apart, without opening them.

PRESENTATION:
Hand two safety pins to a spectator and have him link them together. Be sure he does not link them through the small opening. Take the pins from the spectator.

With thumb and forefinger of your left hand, take hold of one of the pins by the small end, with the opening of the pin facing upward. With your right hand, take hold of the other pin, maneuver them in position as in figure 1.

Notice the position of pin "A" to that of pin "B". The opening of pin "A" is upward. As pin "B" is pulled downward pin "A2 will open. Try this slowly at first, you'll get the idea.

When ready to perform, the action must be fast and deliberate.

FIGURE 1

Still holding the pin with your left hand, grasp the other pin by its head with the thumb and forefinger of your right hand. See Figure 2.

180

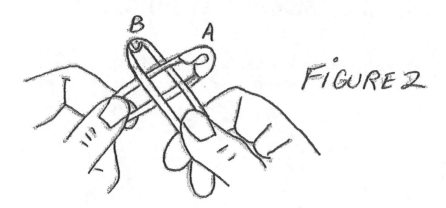

Take a firm grip, as in Figure 2 and pull them apart with a sudden jerk. See Figure 3.

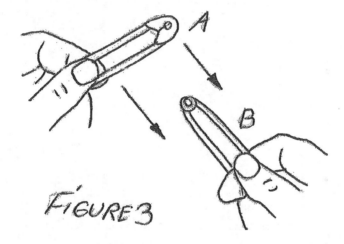

The sudden opening and closing of pin A cannot be seen by the naked eye.
Hand them to the spectator for examination.

IT SOUNDS BROKEN

Place a tooth pick in a handkerchief and hand it to a spectator in such a way that he can feel it with his hands. Ask him to break it as many times. When handkerchief is opened, the toothpick is show to be intact.

MATERIAL:
A man's white pocket handkerchief with borders. Toothpicks round or flat.

PREPARATION:
Place a toothpick into the hem of a handkerchief. (Figure 1)

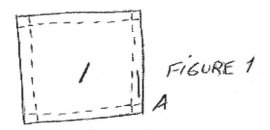

Place this handkerchief, folded up, in your pocket without bending the toothpick.

PRESENTATION:
Remove the handkerchief from your pocket, and grasp it with the fingers of the right hand by corner A, thus hiding the secret toothpick. Stroke the handkerchief down ward with the other hand, two or three times.
Maintain hold on side "A", and open out the handkerchief. Show and place toothpick in center of handkerchief. Fold handkerchief over toothpick I such a way, as to bring the secret toothpick to the center, which is hidden by the folds. (Figure 2)
Have spectator feel the tooth pick through the folds and have him break it once or twice.

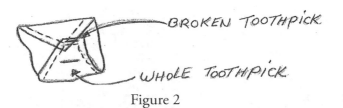

Figure 2

Re-open handkerchief and let the restored toothpick fall out.

➤ TEAR PROOF

MATERIAL:
One safety pin (medium in size) and new;
One man's pocket handkerchief with a good border.

EFFECT:
A safety pin is inserted in the top edge of a man's handkerchief. The pin is suddenly moved from left to right, this will simulate a tearing noise, but upon examining the handkerchief, it is seen to be unharmed.

PRESENTATION:
Insert the safety pin near a corner and over the edge of the handkerchief. The figure shows how pin is positioned.

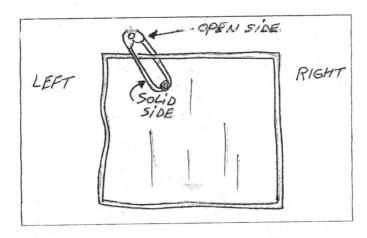

Hold pin by the small end and place pin in position. The pin side faces the right, and the solid side faces left. Pin must be completely over the border.

Have two spectators hold the two upper corners of the handkerchief, take hold of the small end of the pin and swing it parallel to the upper border. Pull the pin steadily and quickly to the right. It will sound as though the handkerchief is being torn. Upon close examination, the handkerchief is found to be restored. The pin is still through the handkerchief and still closed.

WHAT HAPPENS:
As the pin is moved from left to right, the pin opens slightly and closes again upon completion of the sliding motion.

CHAMELEON SHOELACE

MATERIAL:
One black shoelace;
One white shoelace;
(Use the hollow kind. Both same length and width).

EFFECT:
Hold up and show freely a black solace. The lace, at once, changes color from black to white.

PREPARATION:
Make small openings right near the two tips of the black shoelace. Insert the tip of the white shoelace into one opening and thread it all the way through the black shoelace up to its tip. Bring the tip of the white lace through at one end.
Cut off the tip of white lace at other end, and sew this end to the black lace. See figure.

Cut off the tip of the white lace at the other end, and sew this end to the black lace.

PRESENTATION:
Hold up the prepared lace with thumb and forefinger of left hand, covering the two tips, and allowing the rest of the lace to hang free. Call attention to the color black. Now, enclose the end with your right fist. With the fingers of the left hand grasp the protruding tip of the white lace, and holding the end of the black lace with the right hand, slide the hand down rapidly. This will pleat the black lace down into the right fist, thus hidden from view. Tug the lace with both hands, role it up and put it away.

THE BURNED MATCH

MATERIAL:
One book of matches.

EFFECT:
Open a book of matches and have the spectator count them and remember the amount. Remove one match and strike it on side of box. Let the match completely burn. Pick up ashes and rub them on the match book. Open the book, the match is found to be restored and well attached. The amount remains the same.

SECRET:
Hold the book of marches as in figure 1. One match is bent and hidden by the thumb of the left hand.

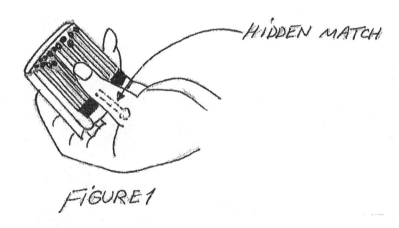

HIDDEN MATCH

FIGURE 1

Right hand removes one match in the vicinity of the hidden one. The book is swung inward into the palm of the left hand, thus replacing the hidden match inside. As this happens the lid is swung closed and secured. This is one continuous action which provides you with good subterfuge. Figure 2 shows book closed with hidden match inside.

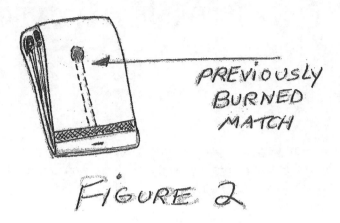

PREVIOUSLY
BURNED
MATCH

FIGURE 2

Strike the match and let it burn completely. Pick up the ashes and rub them on the cover. Open the book and show the match restored. Have the spectator count them. It is found to be the same amount, as before.

THE MARKED MATCH

MATERIAL:
A book of matches;
A Sharp pencil.

EFFECT:
One of three paper matches is marked by penciling a line on it. The spectator is asked to pass anyone of the three matches under the table to you, who, without looking, tells the spectator which match is marked.

PREPARATION:
Prepare a packet of matches, as follows.
Hold the end match by the head with one hand and the match case with the other. Proceed to twist the match back and forth to loosen its fibers. Replace packet into your pocket, and you're set to go.

PRESENTATION:
Tear out three matches from a packet, be sure that one of the matches is the prepared one. With a sharp pencil, mark the stem of the prepared match by drawing a line on both sides. (Figure 1)

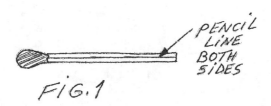

Hand the spectator, sitting opposite you, the three matches. Have him pass anyone of the matches to you under the table, and you will tell him, without looking, whether it is the marked or not. Remember, the marked match is the one that's twisted, the normal one's are stiff. See figures.

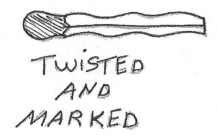 

➢ SUGAR AND ASHES

MATERIAL:
Sugar cubes, from a dinner table;
Some cigarette ash.

EFFECT:
The spectator is challenged to light a sugar cube, but fails to do so. You then display tins magical power and by effecting this feat.

PRESENTATION:
Before you begin, have with you some cigarette ash. Pay no attention to it, this will be unnoticed. Pass out several lumps of sugar to your guests, and say, "this sugar is for a magical experiment". Have them light their cubes with a match, and that the cube must burn with a flame. The guests try this, bust are completely unsuccessful. The sugar will melt, but with no flame.

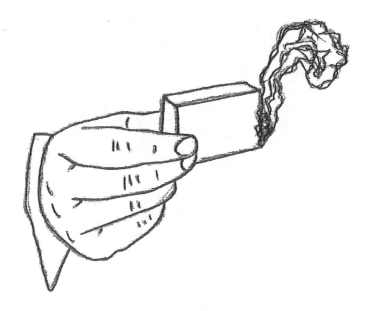

Ask someone to pass you a cube of sugar, place a small amount of ashes which are hidden in your hand or otherwise resting on the table, to one comer of the cube.
Remove a match and proceed to light it. The ashes act as a catalytic agent.

THE UNBENDABLE SPOON

EFFECT:

A spoon is apparently bent by the performer, but as scan as it is brought to view, it is seen to be in perfect condition.

PRESENTATION:

(While sitting at the dinner table)

Hold the spoon by its handle with both hands, the handle pointing at you, the scoop of the spoon resting on the table. In holding the spoon, keep the backs of the hands up, one over the other. The little finger of the lower hand, the hand near the spool, under the handle. (Figure 1)

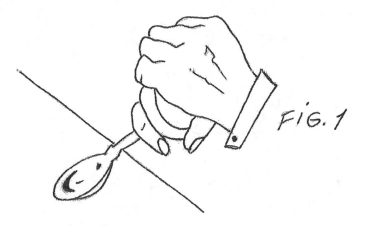

FIG. 1

Pretend as if bending the spoon handle upward. Keep in mind that this is only a simulation. Slowly bring the hands to a vertical position to the spoon. Remove the upper hand and lift the spoon off the table as if you are holding the bent end with the other hand. The little finger does the lifting. Part of the hand hides the end of the spoon. Drop the spoon on the table to show that it has not been bent.

➢ BANANA TWINS

(A table gag)

This funny gag must be prepared before you begin, and must be unknown to anyone.
Leave the prepared banana with the rest of the fruit, in the fruit bowl. This effect will take its own course, make no mention to it.

MATERIAL:
A bunch of bananas;
One needle;
Some thread.

EFFECT:
One of two bananas, is cut in half. When the other banana is peeled, it, too is cut in half.

PREPARATION:
Try to obtain two bananas attached to a single stalk. They should be as much alike as possible.
Prepare one banana as follows. Run a threaded needle through the ski, perpendicular to the length of the banana, about the middle of its body. (Figure 1)

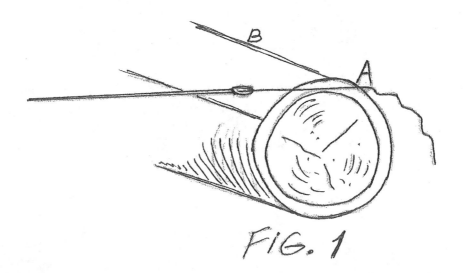

FIG. 1

At this point, as with the others, do not pull the thread all the way through, but allow for sufficient length, so that about two or three inches of thread remain at puncture "A".

Run the needle through again, starting at the second puncture, "B", and ending at a new puncture, "C". (Figure 2)

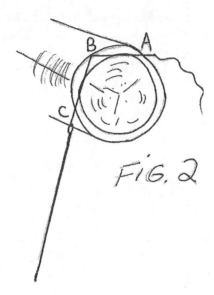

FIG. 2

Continue around the banana, to "D" and "E", until you complete a polygon of thread. (Figure 3)

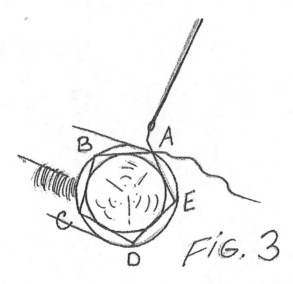

FIG. 3

The thread must exit from puncture A. Pulling both threads at this exit will cut the banana in half at this point without cutting the skin. The holes left from the needle will not be visible. Leave on table with other fruits and wait for the laughs.

THE MAGICAL BAKER

Here is a sure way of getting some hilarious laughs, wow's and applause. If there happens to be someone with a hat all the better for you, if not, have ready a container that is similar in size and width. In our explanation we will refer to the hat.

MATERIAL:
½ or 1 pint of milk in its own container;
One egg;
Salt;
Sugar;
Spoon;
One roll of transparent tape.
One aluminum can;
One glass or plastic tumbler (This must fit inside the aluminum can; the diameter slightly less than the can).

PREPARATION:
The aluminum can must be open at one end. Remove any paper wrapping from the can and write the word "Flour" across the can. Turn the can around and drill a hole close to the top and large enough to cover the base of your thumb. (Figure 1)

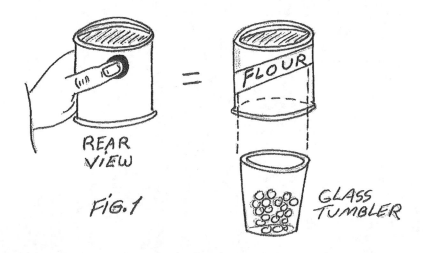

REAR VIEW

FIG. 1

FLOUR

GLASS TUMBLER

Prepare the tumbler by filling it with small pastries. Cover the tumbler with the can, the hole toward you. Rest these on your table along with the milk, egg, sugar, salt and a spoon.

Now begins the action.

Ask to borrow a hat from your spectator. If not available use the container, previously mentioned.

Figure 2 shows the connect way to hold the hat (container).

Notice the can and the tumbler inside.

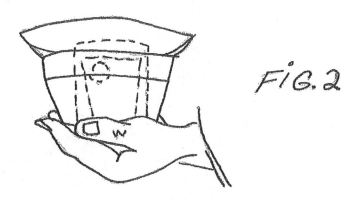

FIG.2

Loaded hat held in right hand.

To show the hat empty, remove the can and tumbler as one. Place the right thumb on the hole and fingers around the can and lift. See illustration above.

This way the tumbler will not fallout, due to a slight inward pressure from your thumb and fingers. It will appear a though you've just lifted the can to show all is fair and empty. Let's start with the flour. (The gimmicked can).

As you show to the audience, that the can will fit in the hat, leave the tumbler inside the hat and incline the can by about 180 degrees, as you're about to introduce the flour. In reality, you pretend to pour the flour into the hat. This action is covered by the brim of the hat.

The label is towards the audience.

Also, be sure that the spectators do not glimpse the open part of the can. (Figure 3)

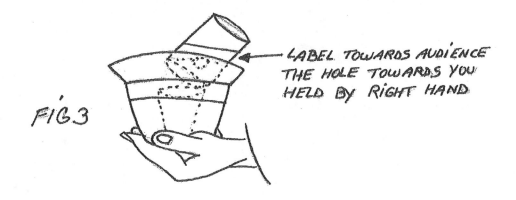

FIG 3

LABEL TOWARDS AUDIENCE THE HOLE TOWARDS YOU HELD BY RIGHT HAND

Place can on table with the label in front.

Remove the top of the salt shaker and apply a small piece of transparent tape on the inside. This will prevent the salt from flowing. Next, pretend to sprinkle salt as the next ingredient. Pick up the spoon and pretend to stir, causing the tumbler to fall. The sweets will now be in the hat.

Pretend to taste the mixture by insetting your finger in the hat, while turning the tumbler right side up, (mouth upwards). Here comes the visual climax. Be very careful with this. I suggest that it be practiced a few times.

Say to the spectators, "and now for the sugar".

You actually do pour some sugar in the hat, really in the tumbler. "Now an egg and some milk". Break the egg and pour the milk into the hidden tumbler. (Figure 4)

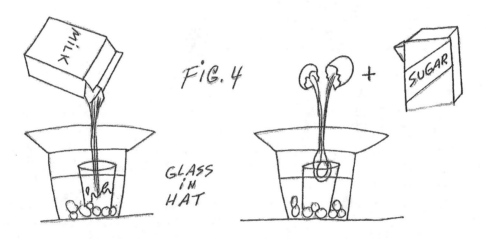

Pick up the can and without saying a word place it in the hat covering the tumbler.

Pause a moment, then say "no, I better not". Take the can out with the tumbler and place it on the table. Make some magical passes with your hands over the hat. Turnover on tray and hand out the goodies.

ILLUSIONS MADE EASY

THE WHERE AND HOW ON CARTONS

Large cartons may be obtained from Department Stores that handle furniture items such as T.V. Sets and so forth. In most large cities there are factories that manufacture cartons and they can supply you with large cartons as well as large sheets of carton material. with these sheets of material a razor blade and some gummed tape, you can make just about anything you need.

In sealing the corners of cartons which will be folded flat for carrying, use a double thickness of tape so that it will wear well. When a carton is to have no bottom or top, and where ever there is an open edge, seal this joint with tape for protection and longer wear. This will also add to the natural look when you must use a piece of tape to hinge a flap.

THE SWORD BOX

Placing an assistant in a box and then thrusting swords through the box at all angles has always been a very perplexing illusion.

Here, we make use of the versatile carton for the box and one quarter or one half inch wooden dowels for the swords. The carton should be of such a size that it will just accommodate your assistant in a sitting position. Small holes are cut in the carton at the point where the dowels will penetrate. Eight dowels will be needed.

Introduce your assistant, and then have her step into the carton, she faces the audience. She then sits down in this position, still facing the audience. This is very important to the illusion.

Once she is seated and out of sight of the audience, she turns sideways to the audience. The top of the carton is closed. As far as the audience is concerned, she is still sitting facing them. If you now take a dowel and push it through the carton from the front to the rear, and directly in the center it would have to pass through her if she were still facing front. Since she is sitting sideways, it passes in front of her stomach. The illustration shows how the eight dowels are placed through the carton. This is a Side View for clarity. You will notice that one goes down through the center, passing in front of her face and down through her legs. There are placed straight through from front to rear. Four are then crisscrossed. It would seem inconceivable that anyone could be in the carton.

After the dowels are. removed, your assistant turns face front again and rises from the carton in this position. We might add that your assistant can help guide the dowel through the holes from inside.

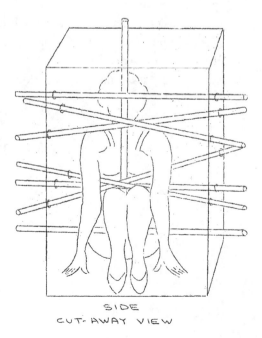

SIDE
CUT-AWAY VIEW

197

DOLL HOUSE

The doll house has long been a favorite of club, plate form, and stage magicians. If you were to buy one of the standard it would represent a considerable investment. We believe you will find this one to be even more baffling than the standard versions. It has the advantage of being light weight and packing flat. The house, when fully constructed, (it is built up right in front of the audience from flat pieces. It is thirty inches long by twenty four inches wide and forty inches high. These dimensions were figured for a girl about five feet two inches tall. For a taller girl, enlarge the dimensions accordingly. The house is constructed from three separate pieces. The front and one side are permanently hinged together. Take other side is hinged to the back. The roof is the third piece. Small pin hinges are attached to the two wall sections to fasten them together when they are assembled.

A glance at the illustrations will clarify the construction details and the method by which the girl gets into the house.

At the start the roof is standing on end; as illustrated. The girl is concealed behind it. The two wall sections are folded flat and leaning against the roof. The illusion is, now ready for presentation.

First, show a large sheet of canvas or other cloth and spread it on the floor. This precludes the idea of traps in the floor. On this, set up the front arid sides section. Now, take the next sections, side and back, and in placing the side up to the front allow the back to swing out, so that it overlaps the edge of the roof as you fasten the side to the front. The girl can then sneak from behind the roof into the house proper without being seen. Next, pick up the roof and show it and, after swinging the house back in placed and fastening it, place the roof on top. The illusion can now be brought to a climax. At your command or signal the girl tips the roof to the rear and stands up in, the house t thus making her appearance.

The wearing of a very full formal gown by your assistant will enhance the illusion and make it look even more impossible for the house to have contained her.

Of course you may paint this Victory house to look like a regular doll house, but we prefer to leave it plain.

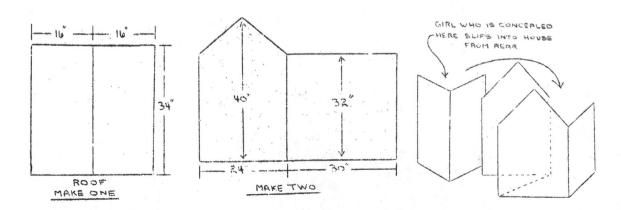

198

GIRL PRODUCTION

This illusion has enjoyed, tremendous success and all those who have been wise enough to try it have raves over the sensation it creates.

You will need two large cartons for this illusion. The tops and bottoms of both cartons are removed and the edges are reinforced with tape. One of the cartons if faked by cutting a large opening into the rear of it. This opening should be plenty large enough for your girl assistant to pass into the carton. Reinforce the edges of this opening with paper. The un faked carton should be just slightly larger than the faked one so that it can be slid down over it. Have both cartons folded flat and leaning against a chair. The faked one is to the front with the hole to the rear. The girl is concealed behind the cartons as shown in Figure 1. Pick up the front Barton and show that it is flat. Now, open it into a box and set it down so it overlaps the remaining carton. The hole or opening if to the rear. As this is done, the girl slips from behind the remaining folded carton and into the open one through the opening in the rear, Figure 2. You then pick up the second carton. Show it. Open it out. Then slide it down over the faked carton. as shown in Figure 3. This, of course, covers the hole in the inner carton so the nested cartons may be turned all around while still on the floor to show all sides. You then clap your hands and the girl pops out as in Figure 4.

Bill Neff uses this method. He picks up the front carton, shows it and. forms it into a square carton. Just as he places it down IN FRONT of the folded one he picks up the folded one. This leaves the girl behind the faked carton. She can then slip inside of the faked carton while he shows the un faked one. This is a very effective move if practiced and worked smoothly.

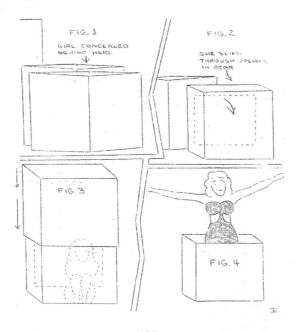

FIG. 1
GIRL CONCEALED
BEHIND HERE

FIG. 2
SHE SLIPS
THROUGH OPENING
IN REAR

FIG. 3

FIG. 4